FOREWORD BY THE LORD CHANCELLOR

The Right Honourable the Lord Mackay of Clashfern

In December 1993 the Government published a Consultation Paper entitled *Looking to the Future - Mediation and the Ground for Divorce*. At the end of my Foreword to that Paper I said that the Government looked forward to receiving constructive comments from which a satisfactory way forward could be derived. I am happy to say that a considerable number of comments were received on the Paper and, having taken them into account, the Government has decided to publish this White Paper setting out its views on this difficult issue.

There have been worries that these proposals are to make divorce easier. At first glance this might seem to be the case. At the moment couples who divorce following a period of separation have to prove when petitioning that they have been apart for two years before they can be granted a divorce. Under the new procedures set out in this White Paper divorcing couples will have to wait for one year in order to obtain a divorce. But the fact of the current position is that **three quarters** of divorcing couples do not opt for two years' separation but cite intolerable behaviour or adultery in order to gain their divorce in just a few months. These people will now have to wait at least a year.

This year-long pause for reflection might be used in many ways but I hope that during this period some will change their minds about going through with divorce. All will be offered the services of a mediator, with whom they will discuss the arrangements following divorce for children, finance and property, and will be able to settle these matters as amicably as possible.

Divorce is an issue of great concern to many, in which moral and religious views are vitally important. Personally I strongly adhere to the view that marriage should be for life. I believe that a husband and wife with such an ideal should provide the most stable and secure background for the birth and development of children. However, I recognise that the civil law must accommodate many situations which, although less than ideal, do occur in practice and I think the reference I gave in my foreword to the Consultation Paper to the teaching of Jesus

(Mark's Gospel, chapter 10 at verses 4 and 5) supports this responsibility for the legislator. In the light of these considerations the framework proposed in the White Paper is, in my opinion, the best that can be devised. It gives the Court an ultimate discretion to refuse a divorce when to grant it would cause grave financial or other hardship. It gives the parties a period for reflection and consideration of their future and the future for their children before allowing them to be divorced. I believe it gives the best opportunity of saving saveable marriages and of minimising the bitterness and damage which the breakdown of such an intimate relationship causes. It gives to the children of broken marriages the best chance of a good continuing relationship with both parents which a divorce process can afford.

I consider we have a heavy responsibility to ensure that our law recognises the importance of the institution of marriage and also to ensure that it does not impose unnecessary damage on the personal relationships with which it deals, particularly those of parents with their children.

Mackay of Clashfern C

Preface

The key aspects of the Government's proposals are that they will:

➤ review present arrangements for marriage preparation;

➤ examine how couples with marital problems can be encouraged to seek help as early as possible;

➤ ensure greater integration of Government policies supporting marriage with those on divorce;

➤ require couples to attend a compulsory information-giving session before starting the divorce process;

➤ remove the incentive for couples to divorce quickly by making allegations of fault;

➤ require a 12 month period for reflection on whether the marriage can be saved – better protection for domestic violence victims will be available during this period;

➤ require couples to think through and face the consequences of divorce before it happens;

➤ ensure that arrangements for children and other matters are settled before divorce is granted;

➤ allow divorce to be barred where the dissolution of the marriage would cause grave financial or other grave hardship; and

➤ introduce comprehensive family mediation as a part of the divorce process.

The benefits of these proposals are that they will:

➤ ensure that couples whose marriages are in difficulty will be better informed about the options available to them;

➤ introduce a system that is better at identifying saveable marriages;

➤ facilitate referrals to marriage guidance when couples believe there may be some hope for the marriage;

➤ make available every opportunity to explore reconciliation even after the divorce process has started;

➤ ensure that there is an adequate period of time to test whether the marriage has genuinely broken down;

➤ remove the acrimony and hostility inherent in the current divorce process;

➤ minimise conflict and so reduce the worst effects of separation and divorce on children;

➤ help and protect children by encouraging parents to focus on their joint responsibility to support and care for their children;

➤ encourage couples to meet the responsibilities of marriage and parenthood before the marriage is dissolved;

➤ allow couples to make workable arrangements through family mediation in respect of their children, home and other matters following separation or divorce.

Contents

Foreword iii

Preface v

Chapter Page

1 Introduction 1

Background 1
Nature and Treatment of Consultation 1
The Present Review 3
The Current Law 3

2 The Main Arguments for Change and Summary of Proposals 6

Introduction 6
The Present Law in Practice 6
Criticisms of the Current Divorce Law 8
The Need for Reform 13
Conclusion and Proposals 13

3 What should Divorce Law and Procedures Seek to Do? 17

Divorce Law and Its Relationship with Marriage 17
The Government's Objectives 18
Other Objectives 20
Conclusion 21

4 Options for Change 22

The Ground for Divorce 22
The Main Features of the Law Commission
    Recommendation 24
Related Areas of the Law of Divorce 32
Judicial Separation 34
Financial Provision in the Magistrates' Courts 35
Nullity 35

5 Family Mediation 37

Introduction 37
The Usefulness of Family Mediation 37
The Case for Increased Use of Mediation 39
Family Mediation as an Integrated Part of the
    Divorce Process 42
Conclusions 44

6   Organising and Paying for Mediation   47

The Government's Decisions in the Light of
   Consultation   50

7   How the New System Will Work   56

Part A - Initiation of the Divorce Process   56

   Information campaign   56
   Provision of general information   57
   Specific information   59

Part B - Divorce Procedures   63

General Principles   63
Other Matters: 65
   Obligation of legal advisers to advise
     clients of other services   65
   Which court?   65
   Power for court to refer for explanation of
     family mediation   66
   Protection of mediation from disclosure
     in evidence   66
   The role of the court in respect of
     mediated agreements   67

Part C - Pilot Project   68

**8   Extension of Proposals to Family
    Proceedings Other than Divorce**   69

Availability of Mediation   69
The Information Session   69

**9   Reform of Related Areas of Family
    Law and Procedures**   70

Domestic Violence Remedies   70
Financial Provision Following Divorce   71
Ancillary Relief Procedures   71
**Practice Direction by the President of the Family
   Division**   71
Lord Woolf's Review of Civil Court Procedures   72

10   Conclusion   73

Appendices

74

Appendix A: Summary of Consultation   74

Appendix B: Questionnaire attached to the
              summary of the consultation paper   108

Appendix C: Bibliography   114

Chapter 1

Introduction

Background

1.1 In December 1993 the Government published a Consultation Paper entitled *Looking to the Future - Mediation and the Ground for Divorce.* That paper presented a number of suggestions about how the process of obtaining a divorce in England and Wales might be improved, and invited comments from consultees in response to a variety of questions arising from those suggestions.

1.2 The response to the Consultation Paper has been very considerable, including a number of lengthy and detailed arguments presented by groups and individuals with professional and personal experience of the current divorce process. An analysis of these responses is provided at Appendix A. In this White Paper the Government presents its detailed proposals for mediation and reform of the law and procedures surrounding divorce in England and Wales, which have arisen out of the Government's careful consideration of all the responses.

1.3 The Government has received clear indications of dissatisfaction with the current system, and considerable desire for reform. These concur with the responses received by the Law Commission during its own consultation period in 1988.

Nature and Treatment of Consultation

1.4 The Government's consultation on these matters has been extensive. There have been three major strands to this consultation, namely, the responses to the Consultation Paper, the answers given on the Questionnaire that accompanied copies of the summary of the Consultation Paper, and the public opinion survey commissioned by the Lord Chancellor's Department as part of the consultation process, and carried out by MORI.

1.5 The responses to the Consultation Paper came predominantly from individuals and organizations with considerable experience in the field of family law. Few of these responses gave attention to all the matters raised in the Consultation Paper, and many raised arguments that did not relate directly to questions posed in the paper. Most responses instead focused on particular aspects of the system, and presented information and argument from an individual standpoint. It is unhelpful and inaccurate to present such qualitative and rich material in the form of percentage agreement or disagreement. Consultees frequently posed questions of their own, rather than adhering to the framework of questions presented in the paper. In these circumstances, a careful evaluation of the substantive arguments is more informative and relevant.

1.6 By contrast, the survey carried out by MORI predominantly required consultees to answer either 'yes', 'no' or 'do not know'. This data is more suited to presentation in the form of percentage agreement, as is the data obtained from the more straightforward questions in the Questionnaire.

1.7 There is thus a balance to be struck between presentation of predominantly qualitative information, such as that obtained in the responses to the paper, and quantitative information, such as that obtained in MORI and some aspects of the Questionnaire. A detailed analysis of all three strands of the consultation is provided at Appendix A. In the main substance of this White Paper, however, the results of consultation are frequently mentioned, and some explanation of these references is necessary at the outset. When drawing together the three strands it has been possible to identify three broad categories of response on particular issues. On some questions there was overwhelming support for a particular course of action, or agreement with particular suggestions. On other questions there was little disagreement expressed, but the support, although clear, was less emphatic. Finally, on some questions the responses indicated a clear divergence of opinion. The White Paper attempts to present the results of consultation in a way that makes clear the nature of response on each particular issue.

The Present Review

1.8   The Government's consideration of divorce law and procedures continues the review of the family justice system begun by the Children Act 1989. The Government's own review follows on from the work of the Law Commission, which published a Discussion Paper in May 1988, and a Final Report and recommendations in November 1990. The Law Commission found that there is considerable discontent and concern about the way the current system is working. The Law Commission's recommendations were discussed at length in the Government's Consultation Paper, and form the foundation of the Government's own detailed proposals, presented in this White Paper.

1.9   Each year in England and Wales over 150,000 couples divorce. The divorce rate is now the highest in Europe. The social, economic and emotional costs of divorce are considerable. Apart from the grief to the couple there is clear evidence that children often suffer greatly as a result of the breakdown of their parents' marriage. The financial costs are high, whether to individuals, the National Health Service, central and local Government or employers.

1.10   The Government is committed to supporting the institution of marriage, and to protecting family life. Nevertheless, however desirable it might be for marriages generally not to be dissolved, some do break down, and, as was stated in the Consultation Paper, the Government is limited in its ability to ensure the survival of marriages, and to influence individual family relationships. The law and procedures for divorce, however, can and do have a major impact on the way people approach divorce, on the way divorces themselves are conducted, and consequently on the way divorce affects those involved.

The Current Law

1.11   The present law dates from 1969. Prior to 1969 the law of divorce required proof of a 'matrimonial offence' (adultery, cruelty or desertion of three years). In 1966 a group appointed by

3

the Archbishop of Canterbury published a report entitled *Putting Asunder - A Divorce Law for Contemporary Society*. This report prompted the Law Commission Report; *Reform of the Grounds for Divorce: The Field of Choice* in November 1966. These two reports paved the way for the Divorce Reform Act 1969, which introduced irretrievable breakdown of marriage as the sole ground for divorce.

■ The ground for divorce

1.12 The Matrimonial Causes Act 1973 provides that there is only one ground for divorce, namely that the marriage has irretrievably broken down. It also states, however, that the person who sues for divorce can only satisfy the court that the marriage has broken down irretrievably by showing one of the following, namely that:

> ➤ the respondent has committed adultery and the petitioner finds it intolerable to live with the respondent;

> ➤ the respondent has behaved in such a way that the petitioner cannot reasonably be expected to live with the respondent;

> ➤ the respondent has deserted the petitioner for at least two years;

> ➤ the parties have lived apart for at least two years, and the respondent consents to a divorce; or

> ➤ the parties have lived apart for at least five years.

■ One year bar

1.13 Divorce proceedings may not be started within the first year of marriage. Incidents during that first year can, however, be relied upon in a petition filed after the expiry of that year.

■ Power to postpone

1.14 A respondent in a two year separation case can apply for postponement of the divorce until the court is satisfied the petitioner should not be required to make financial provision for

the respondent, or that the provision made is fair and reasonable.

■ Hardship bar

1.15 Upon application by a respondent in a five year separation case, the court has the power to bar divorce if it believes that grave financial or other hardship would result from the dissolution and that it would be wrong to dissolve the marriage. In making its decision, the court considers all the circumstances, particularly the conduct of the parties and the interests of the children.

■ The procedure for obtaining a divorce

1.16 Uncontested divorces cases go through under the 'special procedure' rules which were introduced in 1973 and extended to all uncontested cases in 1977.

1.17 Under the special procedure, a District Judge decides whether matters alleged in the petition have been proved by assessing the evidence of the petitioner given by affidavit. If the District Judge is satisfied, a certificate will be issued and the case placed in the Special Procedure List. Shortly afterwards a decree nisi will be pronounced in open court. Six weeks after that the petitioner may apply for the decree to be made absolute which has the effect of legally dissolving the marriage.

1.18 In many cases the arrangements relating to finance and the home are dealt with after decree nisi. Disputes relating to these matters can take up to two years to resolve through the courts.

1.19 When the special procedure was introduced for undefended divorces, legal aid was withdrawn from the conduct of these divorces, although legal advice and assistance became available under the Green Form Scheme. Legal Aid remained available for defended divorces and for proceedings about the couple's children, property or finances. Annual net expenditure on Legal Aid in matrimonial and family proceedings was £332 million in 1993/94.

Chapter 2

The Main Arguments for Change and Summary of Proposals

Introduction

2.1 It was clear from the responses to the consultation that there is considerable discontent with the current system. Many consultees considered that the current divorce law encourages hostility and bitterness by creating an incentive for petitioners to make allegations of fault, regardless of whether these are relevant to the reasons for the breakdown of the marriage. In this chapter, the criticisms of the current system and arguments for change put forward by consultees, are explained. These responses are outlined in more detail in Appendix A, which provides an analysis of the responses on the issues raised in the Consultation Paper.

The Present Law in Practice

2.2 The divorce numbers in England and Wales, although high compared to the rest of Europe, are comparatively stable, having risen by an annual average of 1% during the last decade. Divorce usually affects around 150,000 children every year.

2.3 When, in 1969, the ground for divorce became the irretrievable breakdown of marriage, the law specified the ways in which that breakdown could be demonstrated. These five methods of proof, known as 'facts', include three (adultery, behaviour and desertion) which involve evidence of fault. The other two facts are two years' separation with consent, or five years' without consent.

2.4 The expectation at the time was that the majority of petitions would rely on the fact of two years' separation with consent. This has not been the case. The large majority (about 75%) of divorce petitions are based on adultery or intolerable behaviour, fewer than 20% on two years' separation, and fewer than 6% on five years' separation.

2.5 It has been generally acknowledged that breakdown is not in itself justiciable. The law has therefore sought to provide specific facts by which the breakdown of the marriage can be established. These facts are, in theory, justiciable. In reality they are not. The details pleaded in divorce petitions in support of, for example, the fact of intolerable behaviour, do not need to be corroborated and are irrebuttable. Such allegations are therefore easy to make and easy to establish.

2.6 Many people believe that divorce is difficult to obtain because fault has to be alleged, thus showing good reason for ending the marriage. In reality, fault is not a restraining factor. More often than not allegations of fault serve only to expedite the divorce process since parties who make such allegations can expect to obtain a quick, unchallenged divorce. It can be argued that the present law and procedure provide in reality for easy, unilateral divorce on demand.

2.7 The median time between filing a divorce petition and obtaining a decree absolute when the petition is based on either of the first two fault facts is six months. Some divorces based on these facts can take as little as three to four months.

2.8 Research has indicated that many petitions are based on the fault-based facts not because these reflect the real reasons for the petitioner's decision to seek a divorce but because reliance on one of the other facts requires a longer waiting time before the divorce can be obtained, that is, two or five years.

2.9 The divorce process is only capable of assessing fault in the crudest possible way. The law is ill-suited to engaging in the complex and sensitive factual and moral judgments which, if achievable, would be necessary accurately to reflect the relative blameworthiness of the parties. As a result, the reliance on allegations of fault serves only to increase the sense of injustice that many parties feel.

2.10 Not surprisingly, the subtlety that the facts are not grounds for divorce, but merely evidence of breakdown, is seldom grasped by those who are sued for divorce. The adultery, behaviour and desertion facts are largely based on, and difficult to distinguish from the 'matrimonial offences' they replaced, yet the evidence required is not of the same weight as that which was required before the law was reformed in 1969. Under the old law, a high degree of proof was required and a petition for divorce would fail if the petitioner had connived at the commission of the offence or colluded with the respondent in any way. The position today is quite different. These bars were removed some time ago. The concern of the present law is with evidence of breakdown, yet the trappings of the old, 'matrimonial offence' system remain. These result in needless conflict, unfairness, and a widespread sense of injustice.

2.11 The need to cite evidence in support of an alleged fact has the effect of forcing couples to take up hostile positions from the very beginning, which may quickly become entrenched. Allegations alienate and humiliate the respondent to such an extent that the marriage is seemingly irretrievable. While children are inevitably affected when their parents separate, research shows that it is conflict between the parents which has been linked to greater social and behavioural problems among children rather than the separation and divorce itself.

Criticisms of the Current Divorce Law

■ **The system does nothing to help save saveable marriages**

2.12 There was a nearly unanimous view among consultees that the current divorce law does nothing to save saveable marriages.

2.13 The current system provides little incentive or opportunity for reflection as to whether the marriage has indeed broken down irretrievably, or whether with appropriate help, the couple might wish to attempt to save the marriage. Once the petition has been filed, and the respondent has acknowledged service without intention to defend, the proceedings can develop a momentum to the extent that, as pointed out earlier, parties may be divorced after a period of just a few months, having had few chances to stop and consider whether this is the best outcome for them and their children.

2.14 As a consequence, many argue cogently that the current system is inimical to the saving of marriages. By requiring parties to take up opposing positions from the outset in a way that heightens conflict, the system removes the opportunity for any meaningful review of why the marriage has gone wrong, and limits consideration about the possibility of saving it. Even in circumstances where the parties and their solicitors approach negotiations in a constructive manner, the divorce process nevertheless requires the parties to sue each other, and to make allegations. Although 99% of divorces are undefended, negotiations about children, finances and accommodation are therefore carried out against a backdrop of allegation and counter-allegation.

2.15 The Government believes that at least some divorce petitions, possibly many, represent a 'cry for help', which may not reflect a seriously thought out decision to end the marriage. It is important that the process that follows the divorce petition allows the parties to consider properly whether the marriage has genuinely broken down. Many believe that the current system provides no such opportunities, or indeed that it actively discourages such consideration.

2.16 The system should be better suited to identifying those marriages which can be saved, and should provide realistic opportunities for couples to seek appropriate professional help through marriage guidance or counselling, in order that they might re-negotiate and strengthen their relationship so that the marriage can continue.

2.17 Even when couples are certain in their own minds that there is no hope for the marriage, and therefore decline the offer of marriage guidance or marital counselling, this does not necessarily mean that divorce is inevitable. The divorce process, therefore, should enable couples to consider their future in an environment that allows them to address together what went wrong with the marriage.

2.18 An important proposal in the Consultation Paper was for the introduction of legislation which places emphasis on the value of mediation as a means of making future arrangements with the minimum of conflict and bitterness. Such a process requires each party to accept that the marriage is over before proceeding to address the future of a life apart. In this way, the couple have to deal with issues of fault, acknowledge that the marriage has broken down irretrievably, and take responsibility for the consequences. If the couples show the slightest hesitation about the ending of the marriage, mediation will cease and couples will be offered time and an opportunity to seek more appropriate professional help, such as marital counselling.

2.19 Even in cases where both spouses have been through the process of deciding that the marriage cannot be saved, and have begun to focus on the future, the door to reconciliation remains open throughout the mediation process. The spouses are never required to take up opposing stances, as they are in the present legal process. In the course of discussing arrangements for a life apart, such as matters relating to the children and finance, couples often address matters which have been a source of grievance and difficulty during the marriage. In the course of finding solutions to these problems they may come to realise that there is, after all, hope for their marriage.

2.20 If, despite these opportunities, the spouses persist in their decision to end the marriage, mediation has other important advantages. It enables the couple to resolve some or all of the issues which will arise on separation and divorce. It enables the couple to negotiate arrangements face to face, rather than at arms length through lawyers or by litigating through the courts. This has considerable benefits for the parties and their children. Litigation and arms length negotiation can heighten conflict, reduce communication and exacerbate the stress and hostility arising from marriage breakdown.

■ Divorce can be obtained without proper consideration of the consequences and implications

2.21 As indicated earlier, under the present law it is possible to obtain a divorce in a few months on the basis of an allegation of fault, and there is no requirement to address the arrangements for living apart until the divorce process is complete. Most consultees thought that it would be desirable instead for the system to encourage consideration **before** divorce, particularly with regard to matters of children, the family home and finance.

■ The system makes things worse for the children

2.22 Research has shown that children suffer and are damaged as a result of **conflict** between their parents, whether the parents are living together or apart. Consultees considered that the current system encourages conflict, by providing an incentive to seek a quick divorce on the basis of allegations of fault. In two or five year separation cases where no allegations of fault are made, there are long periods of uncertainty which are damaging to children. Furthermore, many couples who seek a divorce on the basis of consensual separation are forced, for financial reasons, to 'separate' by living as two households under one roof. This gives rise to an artificial atmosphere that is confusing and harmful to children.

2.23 In addition, some consultees said that the current process is 'adult-focused', paying particular regard to the interests of the parents, often to the detriment of the children's welfare.

■ The system is unjust

2.24 Most consultees considered that the current law is unjust. Divorces based on fault are difficult and expensive to defend. In any event, not all 'faults' are aptly described as such. They may be due instead to a mental illness or disability, or simply to incompatible values or lifestyles. The system construes the petitioner as the wronged party, and the respondent as the wrong-doer, yet in the situations described above this would appear to be unjust. Consultees pointed out that the sense of injustice that parties feel will of course exacerbate hostility and bitterness.

2.25 In addition, some consultees noted that the absence of practical opportunities for counselling aggravated hostilities, although consultees did not specify the kind of counselling that they considered would be helpful. The adversarial legal system was also blamed by consultees for increasing hostility and bitterness.

■ The system is confusing, misleading and open to abuse

2.26 Many consultees noted the confusion about the current law, a criticism also noted by the Law Commission. This confusion stems from combining a ground for divorce (irretrievable breakdown of marriage) which apparently does not require evidence of fault, with the need to establish the irretrievable breakdown by reference to at least one of five specified facts, three of which do rely on allegations of fault.

2.27 It was considered that the current law is open to wide-spread abuse because it is not necessary and rare in practice for allegations of fault to be corroborated.

2.28 Of these points, consultees were particularly concerned about the possibility of petitioners making allegations of fault that are exaggerated and uncorroborated, or not relevant to the breakdown of the marriage. As some consultees pointed out, this is another factor that will exacerbate hostility. It was generally thought that the system should be made fairer, clearer and more readily understood.

■ The system is discriminatory

2.29 Some consultees noted that the current system discriminates against those who do not have the financial means to separate and arrange separate accommodation before divorce. The option of relying on the separation fact is thus closed to those of

limited means, leaving allegations of fault as the only alternative.

■ The system distorts parties' bargaining positions

2.30 Some consultees also suggested that, in the current system, the party who does not want a divorce is in a position to extract concessions by virtue of his or her stronger bargaining position. This is particularly the case in separation cases, where the party who does not want the divorce can force the other party to agree to proposals related to children and finance, in return for their consent to the divorce. If the spouse who does not want the divorce withholds consent, the period of separation required before divorce can be obtained will be much longer; five years instead of two.

The Need for Reform

2.31 The previous sections indicate the strong feeling among consultees that the current divorce law is inadequate in a number of serious ways. Consultees said they considered the problems to be sufficiently serious to merit significant change to the present divorce law and procedures. In particular, they mentioned the need to minimise hostility and injustice, and to stop *de facto* divorce on demand.

2.32 Although some consultees considered that it was an advantage that a quick and easy divorce might be obtained, for example in cases of domestic violence, the clear balance of consultation was in favour of change. The Government has therefore decided that there is a strong case for reform of the present divorce law and procedures. In particular the Government has noted the failure of the current system to encourage reconciliation, and its tendency to exacerbate hostility and conflict and so the distress and harm caused to children.

Conclusion and Proposals

2.33 This White Paper presents the Government's detailed proposals for reform of the divorce system in England and Wales. These proposals relate to the law and procedures of divorce, and also to arrangements for extending the use of family mediation as part of the divorce process. The Paper does not deal with the law on property adjustment or financial provision after divorce and the proposals do not relate to Scotland or to Northern Ireland.

2.34 The Government proposes in this White Paper that it should be possible to obtain a divorce in England and Wales on the sole ground that the marriage has irretrievably broken down. The breakdown of the marriage should be demonstrated by the passing of a period of time for reflection and consideration, in order for the couple to address what has gone wrong in the marriage, whether there is any hope of reconciliation, and, in the event that they decide that the breakdown is irretrievable, to make proper arrangements for living apart **before** a divorce order can be made. The Government proposes that the minimum period of time for reflection and consideration should be twelve months. In practice the period may be longer in a significant number of cases, because some couples will elect not to apply for divorce immediately the period has ended, and in other cases the divorce order will be delayed because arrangements for children, property and finance have not been made.

2.35 The period will provide solid proof that the breakdown in the marital relationship is irreparable. It will provide the parties with time to decide whether or not they wish to be reconciled, and within which to resolve practical questions if they decide to divorce. It will not be a purely passive period, during which parties merely wait out the legally required time without any clear objective and without any real attempt to focus upon the dramatic changes that will occur if and when the divorce actually does happen. Instead, unlike the current system, the parties will have to consider the consequences of divorce before it happens. This will entail the often painful exercise of deciding such issues as:

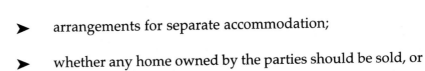

> arrangements for separate accommodation;

> whether any home owned by the parties should be sold, or a tenancy transferred;

> with whom the children are to live;

> how contact with the other parent is to be organised and ensured;

> how the furniture and other possessions should be divided.

This will be in addition to learning to adjust emotionally, socially, and psychologically to the dramatic change in their circumstances and in their lives and the lives of their children. The period may represent a more potent encouragement to some couples to remain together than the current system, which provides an almost automatic passport to divorce, with every encouragement to dwell on the past and ignore the future.

2.36 If spouses are prepared to swear to the belief that the marriage has broken down, and to proceed to make arrangements involving the future care of their children, separate accommodation and the disposition of any property and then, a considerable time later, they reiterate the view that the breakdown in their relationship is irreparable, there can scarcely be any better proof that the marriage is at an end.

2.37 The Government proposes that in future those who intend to commence the divorce process should be required as a condition precedent to attend by appointment an information giving session. This will introduce parties to the benefits of marriage guidance and counselling, provide information about the emotional, psychological, financial and legal aspects of separation and divorce, and its effects on parents and children. The session will provide an important opportunity for the objectives of family mediation to be explained, and the benefits of couples working together on future arrangements to be described. This will result in those who go through divorce having better information about the process from the beginning,

and about the sources of help available to them and their children. In order to support the objective of a wider use of family mediation in the process, the Government also proposes that in future assistance with the costs of family mediation should be available to eligible couples alongside the arrangements for the provision of legal services under the legal aid scheme.

Chapter 3

What should Divorce Law and Procedures Seek to Do?

Divorce Law and Its Relationship with Marriage

3.1 Consultees considered that the law and procedures of divorce should reflect the seriousness and permanence of the commitment involved in marriage. Furthermore, the system should require divorcing couples to consider carefully the consequences and implications of divorce before dissolution was finalised. Divorce should not be so easy that the parties have little incentive to make a success of their marriage, and, in particular, to overcome temporary difficulties.

3.2 Marriage remains the aspiration of most people. Young people today are more likely to postpone marriage in favour of living together. Most will eventually marry with the expectation that the relationship will be for life.

3.3 Rapid social change in recent decades has had an unparalleled impact on family life to the extent that couples often enter marriage with unrealistic expectations, and little, if any, preparation for the complexities of daily living and the demands of parenting. Sadly, few acknowledge relationship difficulties until problems have become very serious, and many couples postpone seeking professional help until breaking point has been reached.

3.4 Consultees recognised that marriage involves mutual legal obligations which other relationships do not. This means that there must be mechanisms to enable people who are unhappily married to reorganise their legal obligations when the marriage breaks down. Otherwise, many will simply leave the marriage and set up a second home and family outside marriage. This was a common occurrence, and a major cause for concern, before divorce law was last reformed in 1969. What the law must do effectively is to provide mechanisms to create an opportunity for reflection and reconsideration and to protect the spouses and their children when things go wrong.

The Government's Objectives

3.5 The Consultation Paper put forward Government's objectives for a better divorce process. These were:

- to support the institution of marriage;

- to include practicable steps to prevent the irretrievable breakdown of marriage;

- to ensure that the parties understand the practical consequences of divorce before taking any irreversible decision;

- where divorce is unavoidable, to minimise the bitterness and hostility between the parties and reduce the trauma for the children; and

- to keep to the minimum the cost to the parties and the taxpayer.

■ Support for the institution of marriage

3.6 The law and procedures of divorce should, as far as is possible, support the institution of marriage. Consultees considered that one way of achieving this would be to require divorcing couples to look to the responsibilities and obligations of their marriage and to consider carefully the consequences and implications of ending the marriage before dissolution is final.

3.7 The Government is aware that a number of initiatives are in place that seek to prepare couples for marriage and to support couples who are experiencing difficulties in their marriage. The Government welcomes these initiatives, and believes that they should be reviewed to see if they can be developed to prepare couples better for marriage, and to encourage those with marital problems to seek help as soon as possible.

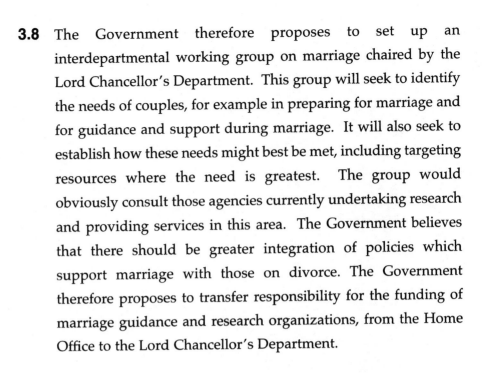

3.8 The Government therefore proposes to set up an interdepartmental working group on marriage chaired by the Lord Chancellor's Department. This group will seek to identify the needs of couples, for example in preparing for marriage and for guidance and support during marriage. It will also seek to establish how these needs might best be met, including targeting resources where the need is greatest. The group would obviously consult those agencies currently undertaking research and providing services in this area. The Government believes that there should be greater integration of policies which support marriage with those on divorce. The Government therefore proposes to transfer responsibility for the funding of marriage guidance and research organizations, from the Home Office to the Lord Chancellor's Department.

■ Inclusion of practicable steps to prevent irretrievable breakdown of the marriage

3.9 Consultees thought that in principle it is desirable that the divorce process should include practicable steps to prevent the irretrievable breakdown of marriage. Some suggested that in practice, however, few marriages could be expected to be saved once one or both parties had taken the serious step of deciding to commence the divorce process. This may be so under present procedures, but it is the Government's belief that a period for consideration and reflection will enhance the opportunities afforded to seek help to save the marriage. While new initiatives may encourage couples to seek help at an earlier stage, the proposals for reform will nevertheless ensure that the door is left open for reconciliation even after divorce proceedings have commenced. The system will thus be more conducive to the saving of saveable marriages.

■ Reduce bitterness and hostility and minimise harm to the children

3.10 Every year some 150,000 children under 16 years of age experience their parents' divorce. As noted in Chapter 2, while these children are inevitably affected when their parents separate, it is conflict between the parents which has been linked to greater social and behavioural problems among children

rather than the separation and divorce itself. A reduction in bitterness and hostility was seen by consultees as a central objective in reducing the harm that might be done to children of the marriage.

■ Ensure that the parties understand the practical consequences of divorce before taking any irreversible decision

3.11 There was clear support among consultees for a reform that would lead to couples having to consider the practical aspects of divorce for themselves and their children as part of the divorce process, before the dissolution of the marriage was finalised.

■ Minimise costs

3.12 Some consultees, especially individual members of the general public, mentioned the importance of keeping the financial costs of divorce to a minimum, whether those costs are met by the couple themselves, or by the taxpayer. Others were concerned, however, that a reduction in costs should not be the sole or primary objective of reform.

Other Objectives

3.13 Some consultees suggested that, in addition to the above, the objectives ought to include a concern for 'justice'. There was, however, a wide divergence in what these responses described, and no clear definition of 'justice' in divorce proceedings emerged from consultation.

3.14 As the Law Commission noted, 'justice' in the context of divorce law has traditionally been taken to mean the accurate allocation of blameworthiness for the breakdown of the marriage. As noted earlier, however, divorce law is only capable of assessing fault in the crudest possible way. Although the law is used to deciding whether or not a crime has been committed, it is much less well suited to making the complex and sensitive judgments which would be necessary accurately to reflect the relative blameworthiness of the parties. In this context, the allegations of

fault, on which most divorce petitions are based, only achieve an increase in bitterness and a sense of **injustice.**

Conclusion

3.15 The Government has therefore concluded that the objectives set out in the Consultation Paper and earlier in this Chapter should be those that guide consideration of the need for reform of the law and procedures surrounding divorce.

3.16 The objectives of supporting the institution of marriage and of taking practicable steps to prevent irretrievable breakdown of marriage, will also guide consideration of initiatives for the better preparation of couples entering marriage and of support for marriages in difficulties.

<table>
<tr><td>

Chapter 4

</td><td>

Options for Change

The Ground for Divorce

</td></tr>
</table>

4.1 The Consultation Paper presented the following options for change to the ground for divorce:

➤ improve the present system with some substantive and/or procedural changes, or with greater use of family mediation;

➤ return to a system based entirely on the matrimonial offence;

➤ a Tribunal or Court inquiry into breakdown;

➤ allow immediate divorce on unilateral demand;

➤ allow divorce on the basis of mutual consent;

➤ allow divorce on the basis of separation; or

➤ allow divorce after a period for reflection and consideration.

4.2 Of these seven options, the Law Commission's recommendation of divorce after a period for reflection and consideration was the single most popular in all three strands of the consultation. No other single option for reform received much support.

4.3 In support of the Law Commission's proposal, consultees emphasised the need to minimise hostility and bitterness, to allow time for marriage guidance counselling, and to make arrangements for living apart in advance of the divorce. Many reiterated the observation that the incentive to make allegations of fault in the present system is not only misleading, but also a source of sterile and avoidable conflict. Preference was shown for a system that placed the emphasis on concentrating divorcing spouses' minds on their responsibilities to each other and to their children **before** the dissolution of the marriage becomes final.

4.4 Some consultees, however, favoured retention of some facts which require evidence of fault, such as adultery, whilst also including facts which do not, that is, a 'mixed' system. This was the only option other than the Law Commission's proposal that received significant support. Those who argued in favour of such a mixed system, considered that the retention of facts which require evidence of fault would help to provide quick remedies for the victims of domestic violence, provide a moral basis for conduct within marriage, and protect 'innocent' spouses while punishing 'guilty' spouses.

4.5 The Government has considered this option carefully. The experience since 1969 demonstrates that, in England and Wales, parties will elect the means of obtaining a divorce that will result in the fastest process, whatever their real reasons for deciding to end the marriage. The Government considers that a mixed system would retain an incentive to seek a quick divorce on the basis of allegations of fault, which clearly exacerbates hostility and bitterness, gives rise to confusion, and makes the system open to abuse.

4.6 It was suggested that if a mixed system were retained, the fault-based cases should be subject to a delay of one year to allow for reflection. This suggestion seems superficially attractive but the Government has decided against such an approach. Delay for a long period following allegations of fault which are considered unfair and unjust by the respondent, would be a festering source of contention between the parties. This would add to the hostility between the parties and exacerbate conflict. This would be likely to have an adverse effect on the parties and damage the children. Nothing would be achieved by such a change.

4.7 Following consideration of the points made by consultees, the Government proposes that the ground for divorce should be the irretrievable breakdown of the marriage as demonstrated by the sole fact of a period for reflection and consideration.

The Main Features of the Law Commission Recommendation

4.8 The Law Commission recommended that divorce should be obtained following a period of time during which the parties could reflect on whether the marriage had broken down, and consider the consequences of divorce before proceeding to take any irreversible decision. If at the end of the period one or both parties so wishes they may apply for a divorce order on the ground that the marriage has irretrievably broken down. The procedures of the new system are discussed in Chapter 7.

4.9 This proposal requires discussion of a number of matters, such as how long the period for reflection and consideration should be, whether it should be capable of being shortened or lengthened in specific circumstances, and whether it should be the same for all couples, or different for those with children.

■ The length of the period for reflection and consideration

4.10 The majority of consultees with a professional or personal experience of divorce agreed with the Law Commission recommendation of a period of twelve months, in the event that the passage of time was selected as the sole fact for the demonstration of marital breakdown. Such a period would be long enough to demonstrate quite clearly that the marriage has broken down irretrievably and to provide a realistic timescale within which to make arrangements for living apart. Members of the general public who had not been divorced typically favoured a slightly longer period.

4.11 The Government proposes that the period for reflection and consideration, which will be required to demonstrate irretrievable breakdown of marriage, should be twelve months. In the view of the Government, this option is the most consistent with the objectives set out in Chapter 3.

4.12 A period of twelve months will provide sufficient time to establish that the breakdown of the marriage is irretrievable, and for couples to make acceptable arrangements for living apart.

4.13 A shorter period will do neither of these, and a divorce could be granted without any adequate reflection and consideration. A longer period would offer no incentive for couples to deal with the past. Not only would it increase distress but it would act as an encouragement to walk out of the marriage, form a new relationship, and take on new family responsibilities before fulfilling the obligations and responsibilities towards the previous marriage and children. A longer period would also result in greater distress to the children, and increase their insecurity about arrangements for their future.

4.14 It is common to attempt to categorise a particular divorce system as 'easy' or as 'hard'. The Government believes, however, that to talk about divorce in these terms is not a helpful way to proceed. Divorce is never easy. The parties and their children suffer greatly whatever the system, and although the divorce system should seek to support the institution of marriage, and to provide realistic opportunities for reconciliation, progress towards that objective may be obstructed by thinking in terms of divorce as either easy or hard.

4.15 Nevertheless, for the majority of those divorcing under the current system, a twelve month period of reflection will in fact make divorce harder in the sense that they will have to wait longer for a divorce. As pointed out earlier, the median time between divorce petition and decree absolute is at present about six months, whereas in the new scheme the absolute minimum period between filing a statement of marital breakdown and being able to apply for a divorce order will be twelve months. For a minority of people, however, the Government's proposals will have the result that they will not have to separate for two or five years **before** starting the divorce process, but the actual divorce process itself will be longer for such parties.

4.16 The Government's proposals will result in a harder divorce process for everyone, in the sense that they will be required to spend time reflecting on whether their marriage can be saved and, if not, to face up to the consequences of their actions and make arrangements to meet their responsibilities before a divorce is granted. For some people, however, this may be easier to cope with because they will not be subjected to allegations of misconduct, or branded as a wrongdoer, justly or unjustly. While the proposals to eliminate allegations of fault will remove the stigma which may be attached to being cited as the 'guilty' party, this should, in turn, minimise the acrimony which allegations of misconduct fuel, so rendering the process less contentious, and less detrimental for children.

■ The relevance of children to the length of the period for reflection and consideration

4.17 Consultees did not favour different periods for those with dependent children and those without. Arguments in favour of requiring a shorter period as proof of breakdown for couples who had no children were that childless couples should be allowed to divorce freely, remarry as quickly as possible and have children sooner rather than later. These arguments were considered to be outweighed by the arguments against such a shortening, that is, that it would devalue marriage by encouraging a casual approach to marriage and remarriage. In any event childless couples and indeed those without dependent children, may have been married a long time and may have complex financial circumstances, in which case a shorter period would not be sufficient to make the necessary arrangements.

4.18 Similarly, arguments in favour of requiring a longer period for those with children were considered to be outweighed by those against. It could be argued that a longer period would protect the interests of children by making divorce harder. It was considered, however, that making divorce more difficult for those with children does not alleviate problems of marital breakdown and such delay is likely to harm the children, especially if the parents blame the children for the delay.

Further, a longer period would discriminate against those with children locked in unhappy marriages. The Government therefore proposes that the period for reflection and consideration should be the same for all couples, whether or not there are dependent children.

■ Should the court have power to abridge the period for reflection and consideration?

4.19 Consultees differed with regard to this question. The principal argument in favour of a power of abridgment was that once couples had made arrangements, they should be allowed to finalise the divorce and proceed with a life apart. Consultees who favoured a power of abridgement also emphasised the need for quick remedies in cases of domestic violence.

4.20 The principal arguments against a power of abridgement were that:

➤ if a function of the period is to provide an objective test of breakdown, then a power of abridgement is illogical;

➤ it would be unfair on the spouse who did not initiate divorce proceedings; and

➤ it would reintroduce by the back door the possibility of quick divorces obtained by allegations of fault.

4.21 The Government is persuaded by the arguments that there should be no power of abridgment of the period for reflection and consideration. The primary purpose of the period is to demonstrate that the marriage has irretrievably broken down, and not solely to make arrangements for living apart. The Government believes that a minimum absolute period is necessary to establish this breakdown with certainty. Any shortening of the period would allow the marriage to be dissolved without having adequately demonstrated irretrievable breakdown.

4.22 Cases where there is a requirement for urgent remedies, such as those where there is domestic violence, are best dealt with under the legislation relevant to those remedies, rather than through

divorce proceedings. A more extensive and wider range of remedies for domestic violence than is currently available is being provided by the Government's current Family Homes and Domestic Violence Bill. It is the Government's view, therefore, that, where they are necessary, proceedings about domestic violence should be pursued under the relevant legislation on that subject.

4.23 Furthermore, the Government believes that a power of abridgement would recreate the possibility of a fast track divorce based on allegations of fault, and give rise to increased litigation over applications for abridgement. This would undermine the principle that the divorce process should minimise hostility and conflict and give parties ample opportunity to reflect.

■ Orders of the court during the divorce process

4.24 The Law Commission proposed that the court should have power, on application or of its own motion, to make orders relating to children, financial provision and property adjustment orders, at any time during the period of reflection and consideration. This is a necessary corollary of requiring consideration of future arrangements before the divorce. Property adjustment orders, however, should not be capable of taking effect until the divorce order has been granted, except where the court is satisfied that there are special circumstances making it appropriate for them to do so.

4.25 Where orders do take effect before divorce however, the Law Commission recommended that property and lump sum orders should be capable of being set aside by the court upon joint application of the parties where they have become reconciled and do not proceed to divorce. Where the order has taken effect, setting aside should only be possible if it will not prejudice the interests of children or third parties. Where parties do not make such a joint application the orders should stand, even if separation or divorce is not proceeded with. These proposals attracted little comment in the consultation. The Government has decided, therefore, to legislate on the basis of the Law Commission's recommendation.

■ Should the settling of arrangements be a precondition of a divorce order?

4.26 Many consultees, especially those who completed the questionnaires and responded to the MORI poll, considered that the making of arrangements for children, property and finance should be a pre-condition of obtaining a divorce order. The predominant reason given was that it was in principle right that the arrangements should be settled before the divorce is granted. This requirement would emphasize the responsibilities of marriage and parenthood.

4.27 The Law Commission, on the other hand, had recommended that making arrangements should not be a pre-condition of divorce because:

> ➤ it might result in both parties rushing to make unsuitable arrangements in order to obtain a divorce as soon as possible;

> ➤ it might result in one party putting great pressure on the other in order to obtain a much better settlement than would be fair; and

> ➤ it would play into the hands of an unco-operative spouse by providing that spouse with a powerful bargaining chip.

For these reasons the Law Commission proposed that the courts should have power to postpone the divorce order in limited circumstances where to do so would be desirable in order to safeguard the interests of those who would be prejudiced if the divorce were allowed to go ahead before arrangements had been made.

4.28 The Government's view is that the settling of arrangements should be a pre-condition of the grant of a divorce order. However, the court should have power to dispense with this pre-condition and make a divorce order, for example where it would be in the best interests of the children that an order be made notwithstanding that arrangements have not been settled. When deciding whether to make a divorce order the court should take account of all the circumstances of the case.

4.29 The Government is concerned that the requirement to make arrangements before divorce should not play into the hands of an unreasonable, spiteful or malicious spouse or provide a formidable bargaining chip for the more powerful or determined party. The Government is also concerned that such a requirement should not increase the demands on the courts, put additional burdens on the legal aid fund or tempt parties to enter into litigation earlier rather than later.

4.30 In implementing this aspect of the proposals for reform, therefore, the Government will wish to ensure that weaker or vulnerable parties and their children are sufficiently protected and that the potential for litigation is minimised.

■ Advantages of the government's proposals

4.31 The Government's proposals will mean that marriages cannot be terminated as precipitously as under the present law.

4.32 The period of reflection is designed to save saveable marriages where possible, and to provide more convincing proof that the breakdown in the marital relationship is irreparable. In situations where the marriage has obviously and irreparably broken down before the period begins, consideration of the practical consequences will be a much more constructive use of the time spent before the divorce is obtained than is presently the case. Where there remains any doubt as to whether the marriage has broken down at the beginning of the period, a more active preparation for life apart will provide a far more cogent test of whether the parties have a future together.

4.33 When faced with the problems of dealing with the practical consequences of divorce, some couples may come to realise that they need to re-consider their position, and, perhaps with the help of counselling, find some way of re-negotiating their relationship so that they and their children can have a future together.

4.34 At the same time, the Government's proposals will help to avoid the major defects in the present law. The damage done by the

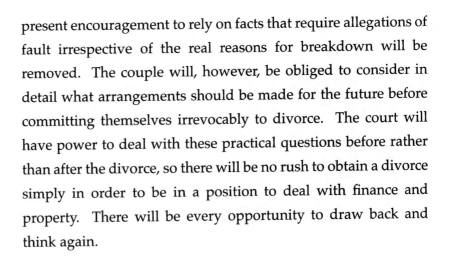

present encouragement to rely on facts that require allegations of fault irrespective of the real reasons for breakdown will be removed. The couple will, however, be obliged to consider in detail what arrangements should be made for the future before committing themselves irrevocably to divorce. The court will have power to deal with these practical questions before rather than after the divorce, so there will be no rush to obtain a divorce simply in order to be in a position to deal with finance and property. There will be every opportunity to draw back and think again.

4.35 The period will allow the parties time to consider marriage guidance without prejudice to their position if they subsequently decide to seek a divorce. This will mean that those who initiate the divorce process as a 'cry for help' will be more likely than in the present system to receive the help they need. The period will provide many opportunities to withdraw from the process in the event that parties change their minds, either as a result of attendance at marriage guidance counselling or for some other reason. The removal of the need to make allegations of fault will help to avoid parties becoming polarised at the outset. The period will also create an opportunity for the parties to consider the arrangements for a life apart before the divorce is finalised, in the event that they decide that the marriage is not capable of being saved.

4.36 The Government's proposals also recognise that divorce can sometimes be a joint decision, responsibly agreed upon between the parties. Many consultees felt strongly that any move towards encouraging and helping couples to take joint responsibility for the breakdown in the marriage, and the consequences that flow from it, would be a positive step.

4.37 As mentioned earlier, research has demonstrated that children are greatly harmed by conflict between their parents, especially if they are drawn into that conflict as go-betweens or intermediaries, as happens all too often in present divorce cases. A divorce process based on a requirement to reflect rather than recriminate will help to reduce conflict and encourage co-operation, which will in turn minimise the distress caused to children.

4.38 The Government's proposals for introducing a wider use of family mediation in the divorce process, explained in more detail in later chapters, will also assist in that aim. These two reforms are complementary. The process of family mediation is more likely to be effective in the context of a divorce process that does not artificially and unnecessarily heighten conflict between the parties. Conversely, the law of divorce cannot provide the help and support that divorcing couples need when coming to terms with the breakdown in their relationship and in the making of arrangements for a life apart. Mediation would provide that help and support.

Related Areas of the Law of Divorce

■ The one year bar

4.39 Under the current law there is a bar on petitioning for divorce during the first year of marriage. It is, however, possible to obtain a decree of judicial separation during the first year, and to rely on incidents that have occurred during that year in a subsequent petition for divorce.

4.40 The Law Commission recommended that a similar set of provisions should apply in the new system. As explained in Chapter 7, the statement of marital breakdown which commences the period for reflection and consideration should be neutral with regard to whether separation or divorce is sought. It should therefore be possible to make a statement of marital breakdown during the first year of marriage, and to apply for an order of separation twelve months later, following the period for reflection and consideration.

4.41 The Law Commission recommended that the effect of the combination of the one year bar and the required period of twelve months' reflection and consideration would be as follows. The parties could make a statement of marital breakdown within the first year of marriage and apply for a separation order twelve months thereafter, but it would not be possible to apply for a divorce unless at the time of application they had been married for two years. If either or both did apply for a divorce within this time the court would not have power to issue the order. The Government has decided to legislate accordingly.

4.42 This may mean that some recently married couples will have to wait rather longer than under the present system before obtaining a divorce. The Government does not think that this will cause any real hardship. It will also help to prevent couples rushing into re-marriage too soon without having had time to think about why their previous marriage was so short-lived. This might help to prevent a subsequent marriage from breaking down.

4.43 As discussed later in this Chapter, a new procedure would be available to enable one or both parties to convert the separation order into a divorce order if they wished, once they had been married two years.

■ The hardship bar

4.44 The hardship bar exists to prevent dissolution of marriage in cases where it would lead to grave financial or other grave hardship for one of the partners.

4.45 The majority of consultees favoured retention of the hardship bar, although there was some considerable support for limiting its application to cases of financial hardship. Many argued that this is the only form of hardship that the courts have ever considered relevant, and that it is wrong in principle to give effect to a respondent's religious or conscientious objections to divorce.

4.46 In contrast to the above arguments, many consultees argued the bar in its current form does provide significant protection from hardship which could arise as a result of divorce, even where that hardship is not financial.

4.47 The Government proposes that the hardship bar should be retained **in its present form.** It would however be potentially applicable in all cases rather than only in five year separation cases as at present. The jurisprudence on the use of this bar is now well established. The Government does not intend to change the present statutory wording or the way in which the law in this area is now applied. Although it is likely to be invoked very rarely, retention will nevertheless prevent hardship arising in a few cases. It may well be useful in other cases as a 'bargaining chip' to the weaker partner, as the extent and usefulness of the bar may not necessarily be clear from previously decided cases. The Government proposes that the hardship bar should be revocable on a change of circumstances. If divorce would no longer cause hardship, it is unjust that the bar should remain.

Judicial Separation

4.48 There was strong support in the responses to the consultation for the retention of judicial separation as an alternative remedy for those who needed to make proper arrangements for living apart, but had objections to divorce, or no wish to remarry. Judicial separation enables those with religious/ideological objections to divorce to achieve a comprehensive rearrangement of their affairs, without ending their marriage.

4.49 The Law Commission recommended that the process for obtaining a judicial separation order should be brought into line with the reformed divorce process, that is, that the ground for both orders should be irretrievable breakdown of marriage proved by the passage of a period for reflection and consideration. The statement of marital breakdown should be neutral. Parties should not be required to state whether they intend to apply for separation or divorce at the time they file that statement. Once the twelve month period has elapsed an application may be made for either a separation or a divorce order. The Government proposes to legislate accordingly.

4.50 The Law Commission also recommended that it should be possible for one or both spouses to apply to have a separation order converted into a divorce order at any time after that order is made. As was explained in the previous section, this power for the court to do so would be subject to the one year bar on divorce and it would remain possible for one party to apply to have the divorce barred on the ground of grave financial or other grave hardship at the time of application for conversion. The Government intends to legislate accordingly.

Financial Provision in the Magistrates' Courts

4.51 Consultees did not comment extensively on the suggestion in the Consultation Paper that it would be unsatisfactory to retain behaviour and desertion as grounds for financial provision in the Magistrates' Court. Magistrates' Courts have power under section 2 of the Domestic Proceedings and Magistrates' Courts Act 1978 to make unsecured periodical payments orders and lump sum orders for a party to the marriage or a child of the family provided that one of the grounds set out in section 1 has been made out. These grounds include:

(c) that the respondent has behaved in such a way that the applicant cannot reasonably be expected to live with the respondent; and

(d) that the respondent has deserted the applicant.

The current grounds therefore mirror those which can be used to establish irretrievable breakdown for divorce. In the Government's view the grounds should be changed to reflect the change in divorce law. This will mean removal of the two grounds listed above from section 1 of the Domestic Proceedings and Magistrates' Courts Act. The Government proposes to legislate accordingly.

Nullity

4.52 Consultees did not view the law of nullity as relevant to a revision of the divorce law. The possibility that the ground for nullity of wilful refusal to consummate the marriage should be

removed because of the need to prove fault was not supported. The Government does not therefore propose to make any change in the law of nullity at this stage.

Chapter 5

Family Mediation

Introduction

5.1 Separation and divorce constitute a painful process for all the family members concerned, but particularly for children. As well as coping with the emotional stress produced by the breakdown in their marriage, the separating couple have to begin to reorganise significant aspects of their lives. Questions relating to where and with whom the children should live, how contact between the children and the non-resident parent should be organised, how the children are to be financially supported and whether the matrimonial home should be sold or the tenancy transferred, are all questions which have to be resolved. These can be very painful issues.

5.2 The legal process and procedures and the means by which arrangements are concluded can add considerably to the stress and pain suffered by the couple and their children. The way in which these arrangements are negotiated can also affect the financial cost of the divorce whether to the couple concerned or, where one or both parties are legally aided, to the State.

5.3 The Law Commission in its Report recommended the use of mediation as a means of couples negotiating their own arrangements surrounding their separation and divorce. The Commission saw mediation as a major element in the development of a more constructive approach to the problems of marital breakdown and divorce.

The Usefulness of Family Mediation

5.4 Family mediation is a process in which an impartial third person, the mediator, assists couples considering separation or divorce to meet together to deal with the arrangements which need to be made for the future. Because the parties discuss these matters face to face, family mediation is much better able to identify marriages which might be capable of being saved than is the legal process. Family mediation can encourage couples to:

- ➤ seek marital counselling if it is appropriate to attempt to save the marriage;

- ➤ accept responsibility for the ending of the marriage;

- ➤ acknowledge that there may be conflict and hostility, and a strong desire to allege fault and attribute blame;

- ➤ deal with their feelings of hurt and anger;

- ➤ address issues which may impede their ability to negotiate settlements amicably, particularly the conduct of one spouse;

- ➤ focus on the needs of their children rather than on their own personal needs.

5.5 Unlike current legal processes, mediation is a flexible process which can take into account the different needs of families, and differing attitudes and positions of the parties. Since one partner may be more prepared than the other for the ending of the marriage, mediation can enable them to plan for the future at a pace which suits them both and within a timescale which does not push them into making hasty and ill-considered decisions.

5.6 Family mediation has as its primary objectives:

- ➤ to help separating and divorcing couples to reach their own agreed joint decisions about future arrangements;

- ➤ to improve communications between them; and

- ➤ to help couples work together on the practical consequences of divorce with particular emphasis on their joint responsibilities to co-operate as parents in bringing up their children.

Mediators are trained to help couples talk about what they each want for the future and to focus on protecting the best interests of their children, even when talking together may be difficult and painful because they are angry, hurt and confused. They are encouraged to talk about the issues in their own way, using language which is familiar, thus enabling them both to say what they want to each other.

5.7 Under the current system, couples need not resolve painful issues until very late in the divorce process. This usually means after the marriage has been dissolved and, quite often, after at least one party has already remarried and taken on new responsibilities. Use of mediation may not significantly reduce the emotional pain of divorce for the couple or their children, but it can help couples to come to terms with what is happening in their lives. Mediation is likely to ensure that, by the time the divorce is granted by the court, important issues about the welfare of children, accommodation, finance and property have been tackled and resolved in many if not all cases.

5.8 Mediation is an alternative to negotiating matters at arms length through two separate lawyers and to litigating through the courts. It can offer couples a constructive framework for using the period between initiating the divorce process and the making of a final divorce order for profitable reflection and consideration.

5.9 An increased use of mediation and the development of its potential would mean substantial changes to the divorce process in order to take advantage of the underlying principles and philosophy of mediation. The mediation process is not concerned with allegations but with issues. It encourages the couple to come to terms with the past, look to the future, meet each other on equal terms, and, with the assistance of a neutral third party, reach decisions about the matters they need to address in relation to the future.

The Case for Increased Use of Mediation

5.10 The Consultation Paper discussed the advantages and disadvantages of mediation, suggested how the advantages might best be maximised, discussed evidential issues, considered whether mediation should be compulsory and invited consultees to comment on these matters.

5.11 Consultees considered that, in general, the advantages of mediation outweighed its disadvantages. Advantages emphasized included the reduction of conflict between the

couple leading to a reduction in trauma for the children. Mediation was also seen to encourage careful thought about the making of proper arrangements especially in respect of children. Questions of professional standards and organization were seen as the key to maximising the benefits of mediation. The Government recognises that appropriate mediation services need to be in place and that mediators are capable of delivering the necessary high quality of service.

5.12 Concern was expressed that mediation should be widely available and that couples should not be delayed in accessing local services. Some consultees expressed scepticism about the cost effectiveness of family mediation, stating that there was a lack of good empirical evidence.

5.13 On the question of whether mediation should be compulsory the different strands of consultation diverged. Those responding to the Consultation Paper and those who took part in the MORI Survey were opposed to compulsion saying that it was a contradiction in terms. In contrast 69% of those who completed the questionnaire were in favour of mediation being a compulsory step in the divorce process.

5.14 The results of consultation indicate that there is a good case for encouraging the use of mediation as part of the divorce process. In addition the research published during the period of consultation also supports this view.

5.15 The research in question was an evaluation of the five pilot studies in the use of comprehensive mediation set up by National Family Mediation (NFM). The evaluation was carried out by the Relate Centre for Family Studies at Newcastle University and supported by the Joseph Rowntree Foundation. Among the many findings of the research, the Government has noted in particular the evidence that mediation is effective at:

➤ reducing bitterness and tension;

➤ improving communication between couples; and

➤ helping couples reach agreement on a wide range of issues.

5.16 Further research carried out at Exeter University (also supported by the Joseph Rowntree Foundation) has confirmed that marital conflict is harmful to children. These findings are significant. The Government is committed to promoting the best interests of children whose parents are involved in separation and divorce. Conflict is harmful to children and the Government is of the view that the reduction of conflict should be high on the list of objectives for a good divorce process. As pointed out earlier, although 99% of the divorces themselves are undefended, negotiations about children, finances and accommodation are still carried out against the background of an adversarial process. Parties are required to sue one another for divorce and in the majority of cases make allegations about each other. The Government believes that this is not the best way of dealing with marriage breakdown.

5.17 It is also important that, where there are children, parents learn early to communicate during the process of making arrangements for a life apart. They are going to have to face each other for many years to come when dealing with contact arrangements for their children and adjustments in these arrangements, when circumstances change. The sooner communication is established and couples learn how to negotiate over such important matters as their children's upbringing, the better. Research shows that the children who do best are those whose parents are able to talk together. It is not good for children to have to act as go-betweens.

5.18 The Government recognises that there are many good family lawyers practising in England and Wales who do their best for their clients, sometimes in extremely difficult and fraught circumstances. Marriage breakdown and divorce are, however, intimate processes, and negotiating at arms length through lawyers can result in misunderstandings and reduction in communication between the spouses. Lawyers have to translate what their clients say and pass it on to the other side. The other side's lawyer then translates again and passes information on to his or her client. There can thus be a good deal of misunderstanding and a good deal of anger about what is said and how it is said. Research has established that communication between a couple is improved by their being able to say things face to face in mediation.

5.19 The Government is satisfied that family mediation is a cost effective means for couples to make their own arrangements consequent upon marriage breakdown. Although the NFM pilot studies show that family mediation is cost effective, scepticism has been expressed about those findings. It was pointed out that the mediators who took part in the pilots were paid extremely low rates of remuneration and that the costings did not adequately take account of the proper add-on costs of legal advice.

5.20 The Government is, however, satisfied that, even when mediators are paid more than they were during the pilot, and when the cost of legal advice is added in, family mediation will still prove to be more cost effective than negotiating at arms length through two separate lawyers and even more so than litigating through the courts. As the use of family mediation increases, so the unit cost will reduce. There is evidence from Australia and the United States that mediation is indeed cost effective. When those countries started to encourage and develop the use of mediation as a more constructive approach to divorce, the available empirical evidence concerning cost-effectiveness was less than is available in England and Wales at the present time. It is doubtful whether further research on the effectiveness of mediation can do more than reiterate the available evidence which is considerable, and supportive of the benefits attributed to mediation.

Family Mediation as an Integrated Part of the Divorce Process

5.21 The Government has reached the view that a greater use of mediation as part of the divorce process will help it achieve the objectives of a good divorce system set out in Chapter 3. Mediation should not be compulsory, but the Government does consider that there should be a definite encouragement to couples to use family mediation. The reasons for this are threefold. The Government accepts that through the mediation process:

➤ marriages which are capable of being saved are more likely to be identified than through the legal process; referral to marriage guidance can occur at any time and the door to reconciliation is always kept open, as spouses do not have to take up opposing stances from the outset;

➤ spouses are enabled to take responsibility for the breakdown in their marriage, can acknowledge responsibility for the ending of their marriage and deal with matters of fault, blame, anger and hurt with the minimum of bitterness and hostility;

➤ couples are encouraged to look to their responsibilities - the responsibilities of marriage and parenthood - and to co-operate in making arrangements for the future rather than focusing on the past and engaging in recrimination.

5.22 The Government is encouraged by the recent research which demonstrates that increasing numbers of couples are seeking to dissolve their marriage as responsibly as is possible. Most want to minimise the hostility, and only a very few want to conduct their divorce acrimoniously. For the most part, couples want to end their marriage as decently and civilly as possible. Mediation offers them this opportunity.

5.23 By focusing on practical arrangements for a life apart during the divorce process, and before the divorce is finalised, couples will be made to face the practical consequences of divorce before it happens.

5.24 The Government agrees that bitterness and hostility are reduced through the mediation process and couples are helped to manage conflict to the benefit of their children and themselves. Communication is improved, making it more likely that arrangements for the children will last, or if they need to be changed by force of circumstances, making it more likely that

the couple can negotiate new arrangements in a constructive manner, and in the best interests of each child.

5.25 In these ways the important objective of minimising bitterness and hostility and reducing the trauma for children can be achieved.

Conclusions

■ Introduction

5.26 The Government recognizes that for the majority of couples whose marriage fails, divorce constitutes a painful and difficult process. It is particularly painful for children. Regrettably no law or procedure connected with separation and divorce can mend marriages or make divorce pleasant, or those going through the divorce process happy. The law, procedures and methods used to deal with the consequences of marriage breakdown can, however, make matters worse.

5.27 The Government is therefore of the view that a more constructive means of making arrangements for a life apart should be made available to couples in the form of mediation.

■ Compulsory mediation

5.28 The Government is of the view that the use of mediation should not be compulsory. Couples should be better informed about mediation and there should be encouragement to use this means of making arrangements. If, however, **both** parties are not willing to give mediation a try, then it is not likely to be successful and valuable resources would be wasted. That would not be in anyone's interests. The Government accepts that mediation will not be suitable in all cases and will not be beneficial to all couples. The research evidence supports this view.

■ Domestic violence

5.29 Particular concern was expressed by consultees that the victims of domestic violence should not be forced to use mediation against their will, and so put themselves at risk. It is clear from what has been said above that this will not happen. If a spouse who has been subjected to violence wishes, for his or her own reasons, to try mediation, then in principle there is no reason why that person should not be allowed to do so. Emerging research findings indicate that not all cases where there has been domestic violence will necessarily be unsuited to mediation. A great deal will depend on the nature of the violence and the dynamics of the relationship between a particular couple.

5.30 Decisions on whether mediation might be suitable for a particular case or couple are best made in consultation with professionally trained mediators. Mediation organizations in this country are aware of the problems created by violence and are addressing these by developing screening mechanisms and are looking at ways in which the safety of clients and mediators can be assured.

■ Children's interests

5.31 Consultees were also concerned that the welfare of children should be adequately protected during the mediation process. Many commented that parents tend to focus on what suits them without regard to whether the arrangements they agree are likely to be in the best interests of their children.

5.32 The Children Act 1989 makes it clear that the welfare of children is of paramount consideration in all matters relating to their upbringing. All those involved in the family justice system, whether as judges, court welfare officers, mediators, or lawyers, will constantly remind parents of this. The Act encourages parents to take responsibility for making decisions relating to their children; there is a presumption in the Act that court orders will only be made if that would be in the best interests of the children. Mediation services in this country are very conscious of children's needs and indeed many mediation services at present offer only child-related mediation. Mediators of course do not act for either party or the child, but are required by their

code of practice to remind parents of their duty to take account both of the welfare of their children and also of their children's views, where these are ascertainable.

5.33 It is clear from work undertaken by National Family Mediation and supported by the Calouste Gulbenkian Foundation that thinking in relation to the involvement of children in mediation is developing rapidly. It is likely that within the not too distant future mediators will be specifically trained to deal appropriately with the interests of children during mediation, and will receive guidance on when and in what circumstances it is appropriate to involve children in mediation.

Chapter 6

Organising and Paying for Mediation

■ The principle underlying the grant of Government assistance

6.1 The Government believes that the costs of dissolving a marriage, like those of forming one, should be borne by a couple themselves. This recognises the responsibility of individuals; it also provides appropriate disincentives against wasteful disputes which merely dissipate a couple's assets.

■ Criteria for eligibility for state funding

6.2 Assistance with the costs of legal help in divorce and ancillary proceedings is currently available under the legal aid scheme, for those of limited means. This assistance is subject to the operation of a merits test. Since the publication of the Consultation Paper the cost of matrimonial legal aid has continued to rise. The annual net expenditure on Legal Aid in matrimonial matters was £332 million in 1993/94, compared with £272.4 million in 1992/93.

6.3 Overall there was general support in the responses to consultation for making the eligibility criteria for mediation services the same as those that apply in legal aid for legal services, namely:

➤ assistance should be subject to a test of financial means;

➤ where they can afford it, applicants receiving publicly funded assistance should pay a contribution towards the cost incurred; and

➤ it would be a condition of publicly funded assistance that those receiving it should behave reasonably in all the circumstances.

6.4 Consultees did, however, have difficulty with the third criterion, requiring 'reasonable' behaviour in all the circumstances. The Government sees no reason why publicly funded assistance for mediation should not be withdrawn if the person receiving it is behaving unreasonably.

6.5 It is the current practice of mediation organizations in this country to ask couples who wish to enter mediation to sign an 'agreement to mediate'. It is clear from the terms of such agreements currently in use, that parties are expected to enter into mediation in the spirit of openness and honesty and co-operation. If in the future one or both parties are state-funded it would seem right that if, for example, one party does not make full and frank disclosure, or attempts to bribe a mediator to influence the mediation process in his or her favour, that conduct would be regarded as unreasonable, should be reported by the mediator and lead to state-funding being withdrawn.

6.6 A rule exists at present whereby lawyers representing legally aided parties are under a duty to report their client if he or she is acting unreasonably and legal aid may be withdrawn. The circumstances in which this rule operates is likely to be different in nature and application depending upon whether the client is mediating or represented by lawyers. However, the principle is the same. Individuals who are state funded should behave reasonably in all the circumstances of their case.

■ Assessment of eligibility

6.7 The Consultation Paper suggested that procedures for a new divorce system might involve persons seeking divorce being offered an interview. It was envisaged that at the initial interview the interviewer would establish whether the individual was eligible for publicly funded assistance for mediation and/or legal advice. It was also envisaged that the interviewer would carry out a preliminary eligibility and means assessment. The interviewer would also be responsible for informing the parties about the divorce process and options available, including an explanation of mediation. Where appropriate the interviewer would refer parties to marriage guidance counsellors, mediators or lawyers.

6.8 The Consultation Paper canvassed several options as to who might best fulfil the vital role of initial interviewer. Included in the suggestions were: Family Court Welfare Officers; local mediation services; or a new independent organization.

6.9 There was no support among consultees for the setting up of a new organization. Consultees considered that this would merely add an additional layer of bureaucracy, and would be expensive. It was considered that it was better to make good use of existing services and skills.

6.10 Consultees did not think that the initial interviewer should be responsible for determining eligibility and deciding when and if state funding should be withdrawn. The person or body responsible for allocating funds, rather than the initial interviewer, should take responsiblity for such matters. Consultees were happy, however, with the interviewer carrying out a preliminary means assessment. Consultees were in favour of parties being better informed than they now tend to be about the divorce process, the options available to them and about the benefits of mediation. They could see an important role for an initial interviewer in this respect. Consultees were concerned that serious conflicts might arise, if an initial interviewer was expected to make decisions about state funding. Consultees therefore favoured the decision-making role about state funding being separated out from the role of information provider.

■ Independent legal advice

6.11 Concern was also expressed about the need for access to independent legal advice and that access to such advice should not be dependent upon participation or refusal to participate in mediation.

■ Advice from same solicitor

6.12 The Consultation Paper also invited consultees to comment on whether a couple who had mediated issues in dispute might consult the same solicitor to obtain advice about the agreement which they had reached. There was a divergence of view on this

matter. Some consultees accepted the proposal. Some consultees opposed it as a matter of principle. Lastly some accepted the proposal reluctantly, but expressed the view that in most matrimonial cases there is by definition bound to be a conflict of interest between divorcing parties which would make advice from the same solicitor inappropriate.

The Government's Decisions in the Light of Consultation

■ Responsibility for allocation of funding

6.13 The Government has decided in the light of the views expressed by consultees that it will not set up any new independent organization responsible for an initial interview and for determining eligibility for state funding in family cases.

6.14 The Government is persuaded that the new system should build on existing services and existing skills. It therefore intends to ask the Legal Aid Board to take on responsibility for dealing with the funding of mediation for those who are eligible for state funding. New legislation will give the Board the power to do so.

■ Initial interview

6.15 The Government also accepts the majority view that the function of information giver should be separated out from the function of eligibility determination and that these functions should be discharged by different persons/bodies.

6.16 Once the function of eligibility determination is separated out from that of information giver, the latter function becomes one which is primarily concerned with: giving information about the options available to couples who are experiencing difficulties in their marriage, the divorce process and related matters; communicating a good understanding of mediation; and explaining the other services which are available such as legal services. These matters are set out in Chapter 7, which is concerned with explaining how the new divorce system will work. The rest of this Chapter will concern itself with mediation, how this will be funded through the Legal Aid Board and with attendant legal advice.

■ Independent legal advice

6.17 As explained earlier, mediation is a process by which couples negotiate face to face about the arrangements for the future with the help of a neutral third party, the mediator. The Government accepts that **mediation is therefore different from legal advice, assistance and representation.** It is likely that most couples going through separation and contemplating divorce will need to obtain good general and legal information, and also will need some specific legal advice about their own legal rights and obligations. They may also need some assistance with the preparation of the necessary divorce papers. This latter type of assistance may, however, be less needed under the new system than at present, since the Government intends that the initial documentation should be much simpler than the documentation required under the present system.

6.18 Given that eligible persons are likely to need some legal assistance prior to and at the time of commencing the divorce process, it is right that state funding should continue to be available for those who are eligible for this type of early preliminary legal advice and assistance.

6.19 If parties decide to mediate, they may well need some legal advice on legal issues which arise during the course of the mediation. Unless some matters remain unresolved through mediation, it should not, however, be necessary for the parties to be legally 'represented' by lawyers in arms length negotiations or litigation.

6.20 Once the parties have reached agreement through mediation, there may again be a need for them to seek legal assistance in translating their agreement into either an enforceable agreement, or a draft consent court order which is drawn up with the terms correctly phrased and which contains terms which are within

the powers of the court. They may also wish to seek legal advice on the merits of the agreement, although not all parties will necessarily wish to do so. The Government accepts that state funding should be available for these limited types of legal advice and assistance as part of the mediation process, subject to a means and merits test.

6.21 The Government does not, however, envisage allowing either uncontrolled access to lawyer **representation,** as opposed to specific advice on specific issues, throughout the mediation process or for solicitors to be employed at the expense of the taxpayer to go over the ground already covered unnecessarily. The Government believes that with suitable quality assurance mechanisms in place, it will not be necessary for lawyers to 'shadow' mediation or, except in rare cases, to unpick mediated agreements. The Newcastle research shows that only very rarely did lawyers interfere with mediated agreements. Most endorsed them.

■ Advice from the same solicitor

6.22 The Government believes that it would be a useful facility for a couple who have reached agreement successfully through mediation to have the option of obtaining drafting advice from the same solicitor in respect of that agreement. This might be appropriate where the couple are happy with the arrangements they have made and have no wish for advice on the merits of the agreement, but require assistance in preparing a legally enforceable agreement or consent court order.

6.23 In addition, there may well also be instances where parties do not want or need advice about their respective rights and responsibilities, but do need advice on how their assets, taken together, may be maximised, for example, the tax and/or state benefit implications of the arrangements they have in mind. This type of advice may be of particular importance to parties who are eligible for state funding where assets and income resources are very limited. Couples who are in agreement about the decision to divorce may also wish to use the same solicitor to

prepare the necessary joint statement of marital breakdown and supporting documentation. The Government will therefore open discussions with the Law Society and the Solicitors' Family Law Association in order to decide how such a facility can be implemented.

■ The nature of funding for family mediation

6.24 The Government's intention is that the Legal Aid Board will grant block funded contracts to local mediation services for the provision of mediation to eligible clients, provided those services can meet the quality standard for mediation work agreed between the Board and a body or bodies representing the mediation profession. These standards would be built on the requirement of the Board's quality assurance system for the solicitors' profession, known as 'franchising'. In effect local mediation services would be 'franchised' rather like firms of solicitors now are.

6.25 Any arrangements to fund mediation must be underpinned by quality standards that will assure good professional practice and value for money. The Government therefore considers there to be a role for a national professional body or bodies for mediators that lay(s) down and enforce(s) as appropriate:

➤ conditions that have to be met before individuals can enter the profession, i.e. a selection, training and accreditation regime;

➤ regulation and disciplinary procedures, including removal from the profession; and

➤ client care and complaints.

These requirements would then form part of the quality standard against which the Board would audit.

6.26 The Government intends that the Board will contract only with mediation services which meet the specified standards. These standards will incorporate requirements that services are affiliated to an approved professional body. The standards will

also specify requirements relating to individual mediators and their membership of an appropriate approved professional body. The Board will audit to ensure that all services and individual mediators within those services meet the quality standard set by seeking objective evidence of compliance with the standards. In some instances that evidence might be provided by the certification of the relevant professional body.

■ Controlling the cost of publicly funded cases

6.27 It is the Government's view that the proposed new system should be able to provide a better service at lower cost than at present. It should therefore be structured in such a way that total costs borne by the taxpayer in providing the information giving sessions, mediation and any attendant legal advice and negotiation or litigation for those cases which do not mediate, will not exceed those which would have been borne by the Legal Aid Fund under the present system.

■ Details of the new funding system

6.28 Since publication of the Consultation Paper on Mediation and the Ground for Divorce, the Government has decided to review the future of publicly funded legal services and intends to publish a Consultation Paper on these matters. As the Legal Aid Board will be responsible for the public funding of legal services within the family justice system and also, as indicated above, the public funding of mediation, it is important that all aspects of the funding process be considered at the same time and not in isolation from each other. The Green Paper on publicly funded services will, therefore, address how resources will be allocated to local mediation services, how the means and merits tests relating to the grant of public assistance for legal services, and for mediation in family cases will be determined, the relationship between the two, the basis of contributions and the applicability and operation of the statutory charge in all cases, including mediated cases.

6.29 The Legal Aid Board will now begin the process of consulting with appropriate national organizations with a view to setting the content of acceptable national standards for mediation and ensuring the auditability of such standards.

How the New System Will Work

Part A - Initiation of the Divorce Process

■ Information campaign

7.1 It is clear that there is a serious need for better information about marriage breakdown, separation and divorce to be made more widely available and to be better understood. The MORI Survey indicated that there was little or no knowledge or understanding of mediation and its benefits and those interviewed were apt to confuse mediation with marriage guidance. The Survey and the Questionnaire indicated that the public would like more information to be made more widely available.

7.2 The Government therefore intends to launch a widespread public information campaign concerned with encouraging those whose marriages are in difficulties to seek out appropriate help in good time and informing the public about the new divorce process. As discussed earlier, couples tend to wait too long before seeking help, and many are ashamed or embarrassed to seek help, seeing this as a public admission of failure. Persuading couples to seek help in good time is a major battle yet to be won.

7.3 It is important for couples whose marriage has irretrievably broken down to be informed about the services which are available to help them and their children, and how they might access these services. The tendency in England and Wales is to use a solicitor's office as the automatic first port of call without first becoming aware of the range of services and the range of options which are available to separating and divorcing couples.

7.4 The Government is of the view that couples need a better understanding of the consequences of divorce and of the effects of divorce on children **before** their marriage is dissolved. A number of services now offer information about the effects of divorce on children and advice on how to explain to children what is happening between their parents and about their future. As discussed earlier, reduction and management of conflict is essential if the effects of divorce on children are to be minimised. It is equally important, however, for parents to be informed about their continuing parental responsibility, what this means, and how to deal with children who are suffering distress as a result of the breakdown in their parents' marriage. In this respect the provision of good information in written and oral form will be an important part of that process.

■ Provision of general information

7.5 The Consultation Paper suggested that there should be a single first port of call, compulsory for anyone who wished to initiate the divorce process. It was suggested that this might take the form of an individual interview during which **information** would be given about services such as marriage guidance, family mediation and legal advice. The interviewer would also give information about the likely costs of these services and about eligibility for state funding. This information would be supplemented by the provision of an information pack which described the services available for couples whose marriages were in difficulties and gave information about tax and benefit implications of separation and divorce, and an outline of the law and procedures relating to divorce. Consultees generally considered that there was a need for published literature to be supplemented with face to face explanations.

7.6 There was support for making attendance at such an interview a pre-condition of commencing the divorce process.

7.7 Several advantages of a compulsory single first port of call were identified:

> ➤ it provides an opportunity to consider whether divorce is the right course of action;

> ➤ it ensures that all persons obtain the same access to information about the divorce process and related matters; and

➤ it raises awareness of support services, and encourages couples to consider family mediation rather than arms length negotiations through lawyers or litigation.

7.8 Concern was however, expressed by some consultees that the provision of information should not overstep the boundary into advice giving. There was considerable objection to an initial interviewer giving **legal advice**, such as a party might expect to get from a solicitor. Some consultees considered that it is not possible to draw a clear line between legal information and legal advice and that what parties want and need at the time they are initiating the divorce process is specific advice about how the law affects them.

7.9 As discussed in the Consultation Paper, legal information, in this context, is an abstract statement of legal principles and procedures relating to divorce and its consequences with general examples of how the law works in practice. Legal advice involves an explanation of how the law applies to the facts of a particular case and the recommendation of a course of action. **This latter would be outside the scope of the information session.**

7.10 Some consultees believed that, in order to be in a position to give good legal information and not overstep the boundary into advice giving, the interviewer would need a wide range of legal knowledge covering many complex subjects.

7.11 Some consultees objected to parties being given general information about the relative costs of different services, expressing concern that this could be misleading and might tempt parties to choose the cheaper course of action without being certain that such a course was the right one.

7.12 A general point made by consultees was that the form of any information given must be entirely objective.

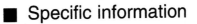

■ Specific information

◆ *Initiating spouse*

7.13 Consultation indicated a wide range of views on the question of who should conduct the interview, and what responsibilities over and above information giving they might have. As discussed earlier, there was no support for the proposal that a new organization be created for this purpose and strong objection to the information-giver being involved in making decisions relating to eligibility for state funding.

7.14 It has become clear that there are several possible models which could be used as ways of communicating important information about separation and divorce and the effects on children. It is clear that face to face explanations are likely to be more effective. It seems that the preferred model for information giving which is in use in Australia and is emerging in most states in the United States is that where a number of parties are brought together at the same time. It would seem that this is more popular with parties than personal interviews which are said to be intimidating and off putting, and which may also run the risk of becoming focused on an individual case which could, in turn, slip into the giving of advice. It is important to note, however, that giving information to a group of people does not imply any suggestion of group work or therapy. It is merely a device for providing objective information face to face in the most expedient, comfortable and cost-effective manner.

7.15 The concept of a group session also allows for a much more sophisticated approach to be taken to the way in which information is presented. It becomes possible to present a wider range of material than would be feasible in single interviews, for example, by use of a well structured video. Use of a video would also provide an opportunity for a larger range of those involved in the divorce process to take part in the presentation and for a wider range of scenarios to be presented. It is likely that the professionals involved will be more comfortable in explaining the services which they offer than in explaining the services provided by others, as would be inevitable if one

professional took responsibility for providing individual interviews. Any video shown should be followed by a discussion with a small panel of professionals representing the main services. There will be an opportunity for those present to ask questions and seek clarification if they wish to do so.

7.16 Experience with this model of information giving is still growing, but the Government's view already is that this model is to be preferred over the requirement to attend an individual interview. No doubt couples will wish to follow up matters on an individual basis, either with a marriage guidance counsellor, a mediator or a lawyer and may well wish to ask for specific advice and assistance on their own position at a later stage.

7.17 The Government therefore intends to legislate to the effect that those who wish to initiate the divorce process by filing a statement of marital breakdown must **first** have attended an information session in accordance with Regulations laid down by the Lord Chancellor. Attendance at the session will thus be a condition precedent to starting the divorce process for person(s) who wish to file a statement of marital breakdown.

7.18 The Government will provide for certain limited categories of persons to be exempted from attendance at an information session, such as the elderly, the disabled or those in prison. Written information will be sent to those exempted. It is envisaged that further assistance may be offered, for example, through a telephone help line, or loan of a video.

7.19 The information available, whether in video, written or oral form will take into account the needs of those whose first language is not English and those who are disabled.

7.20 As attendance at an information session will be a condition precedent to commencing the divorce process, the design and operation of such sessions will be part of the work of the Lord Chancellor's Department, although the Department may in due course wish to contract for the provision of the information sessions.

7.21 It will be essential that the information sessions present a fair and unbiased view of all the services available to couples and of all the options open to them. Such a system should result in couples having a better understanding of the emotional, social and practical consequences of marriage breakdown and divorce. It should also mean that parents better understand the effects separation and divorce have on children, and especially the harmful effects on them of continuing conflict.

7.22 Information sessions will be free of charge to those attending.

◆ Non-initiating spouse

7.23 A spouse who does not participate in the filing of a statement will not be obliged to attend a session before the divorce process is initiated unless he or she wishes to do so. Where a spouse who has not participated in the filing of a statement wishes to comment on that statement, or to make an application on his or her own behalf in respect of children, property or finance, attendance at a session will be required before a response or application may be filed. A non-initiating spouse will be notified of this requirement and given details of the purpose of the information sessions at the time the statement of marital breakdown is served. This will ensure that both parties are well informed about the nature of divorce, its effects on children, and the options available for making arrangements.

7.24 The non-initiating spouse should receive a notice outlining the procedures to be followed during the divorce process, and an explanation of what will happen during the period for reflection and consideration and at the end of it. The procedural rights of the non-initiator should be made clear. For example, the non-initiating spouse should be invited to comment on the factual information in the statement of marital breakdown and its accompanying documents, such as names, addresses, date and place of marriage, details of the children, home, assets, and the basis of the court's jurisdiction, that is, domicile or habitual residence of the parties.

7.25 The Law Commission recommended that the non-initiating party should not be invited to comment on the statement of belief by the initiator that the marriage has broken down. Such an invitation could seriously mislead the other party about the power of the court to make any orders concerning the assertion that the marriage has broken down. What would be desirable however is that the explanatory notes inform the non-initiator that if he or she believes that the marriage has not broken down and that it can be saved, then he or she may wish to contact an appropriate local marriage guidance organization. A list of such organizations, together with telephone numbers could be attached to the notes.

7.26 It will be important that the non-initiating spouse understands the basis on which the marriage may be dissolved. At the end of the full period of reflection and consideration, provided the initiator has complied with all the legal and procedural requirements and these have been checked by the court, the law will presume that the marriage has irretrievably broken down. Unless the hardship bar applies, the court will have to make an order of divorce.

7.27 The Government is of the view that if one or both parties believe that their marriage can be saved, then a battle in court is not the way to save it. Courts cannot save marriages. The parties must do this for themselves. The proposed scheme will give parties time to do so and information about how to seek professional help in so doing. There is nothing effective which the legal system can do in this respect.

7.28 Where the period of consideration and reflection has been initiated by one spouse, and the other spouse needs to file an urgent *ex parte* application under the Children Act 1989, for example for a prohibited steps order, then there would be no requirement for the non-initiating spouse to attend an information session before such an application. Where however such a spouse wishes to go on to ask for an *inter partes* residence or contact order, he or she should attend an information session **before** being heard by the court on these matters unless the court dealing with the *ex parte* prohibited steps order grants leave to do otherwise. In this event such a party should be required to attend an information session as soon as possible after applying for the residence or contact order.

Part B - Divorce Procedures

General Principles

7.29 Annex D of the Consultation Paper, explained the detailed procedural scheme proposed by the Law Commission, which was well received by those who responded to the Commission's own discussion paper and Report. Those who responded to the Government's paper did not comment extensively on these matters.

7.30 Full details of a procedural scheme will be laid down in Regulations made by the Lord Chancellor. The Government has decided, however, that the following principles should underlie reforms to the procedures for obtaining a divorce:

➤ **use of neutral terminology as recommended by the Law Commission:** and no requirement that one party 'sue' the other for divorce;

➤ **initiation:** the process should be initiated by a *statement of marital breakdown,* capable of being filed by one spouse alone or by both spouses jointly, and indicating the belief of the party or parties that the marriage has broken down but not giving any reasons for this; there should be no requirement that the initiating document state that the marriage has broken down irretrievably at that stage and nor should it require the parties to state whether they want a divorce or separation at that stage. The statement should be on a prescribed form and sworn;

➤ **suspension of period of reflection and consideration:** the period for reflection and consideration should be capable of suspension in order to facilitate reconciliation; procedures should also enable the period to be activated again;

➤ **service on non-initiating spouse:** there should be proper means of service of the statement of marital breakdown and supporting documentation on a spouse who has not participated in the filing of those documents. Such a spouse should be provided with an opportunity to file his or her own **statement of facts** (but not proposals at this stage) relating to the children, home and finance but not a separate statement of marital breakdown; details of the information giving sessions should be included and explanatory notes about the procedures to be followed and the procedural rights of the non-initiating spouse;

➤ **application for separation/divorce order:** it should be possible for parties to make an application for either a separation or a divorce order at the end of the requisite period of reflection and consideration. An application should be capable of being made by one party alone or **both** parties jointly irrespective of which spouse filed the statement of marital breakdown or whether this was a sole or joint statement; such an application should declare that the marriage has broken down irretrievably but give no reasons;

➤ **conversion of separation order:** procedures should exist which will enable one or both parties to convert a separation order into a divorce order at any time after a separation order is made. This procedure would be subject to any time bar on divorce and would need to allow for one party to apply for a bar on the grounds of grave financial or other hardship if that were appropriate; and

➤ **timing of application:** the Law Commission recommended that one or both spouses should be able to apply for a separation or divorce order when **eleven months** of the twelve month period had elapsed and that an order should be made by the court one month thereafter. Consultees considered that a full twelve months should elapse **before an application** was made. The Government accepts this view and therefore intends that legislation will provide that once the full period for reflection and consideration, i.e. twelve months, has elapsed an application for a divorce order may be made. The Court will have power to make the order thereafter provided the necessary conditions, for example relating to attendance at an information session and the making of arrangements, have been met and subject to the imposition of any hardship bar.

Other Matters:

■ Obligation of legal advisers to advise clients of other services

7.31 The Law Commission recommended that parties' legal advisers should be regarded as under an obligation, in addition to their ordinary duty to explain clients' legal position, to inform them of other services and to make referrals where appropriate. This duty should encompass marriage counselling and family mediation. The Lord Chancellor will therefore make rules requiring solicitors advising, assisting or representing either party, at any stage in the proceedings, to certify that they have informed their clients of the nature and purposes of counselling and family mediation and the services available in their area, and whether they have referred them to people qualified to offer such services.

■ Which court?

7.32 The Consultation Paper raised the question of whether the divorce process should continue to begin in the Divorce County Court. An alternative would be for it to begin in a Family Proceedings Court. Although few consultees commented on this point, those who did considered that the Divorce County Court was the appropriate forum for initiation of the divorce process. The Government has decided that Regulations laid down by the Lord Chancellor should provide for this.

■ Power for court to refer for explanation of family mediation

7.33 The Law Commission recommended that, although participation in family mediation should be voluntary, the court should have a power to refer the spouses to meet a specified family mediator in order to discuss the nature and potential benefits of mediation in their case. It is possible that in some cases one or both parties will not appreciate the nature and effectiveness of family mediation despite the information session or may not have considered mediation to have been relevant earlier in the process. The object of the referral would be to enable the parties to reach a better informed decision as to whether they wished to participate in family mediation. The specified family mediator to whom the parties are referred, should be under a duty to report back to the court within a given time limit on whether or not the parties have kept the appointment and whether or not they have agreed to take up an offer of mediation. The Government understands that a referral procedure similar to this is in operation in Scotland, and has proven to be effective.

■ Protection of mediation from disclosure in evidence

7.34 The Commission also recommended that a statutory privilege should be conferred upon statements made during the course of mediation. This privilege should attach to the parties rather than the mediator. It follows that statements could be admitted with the consent of both parties. This would accommodate the practice of some types of mediation in which there is both an 'open' and a 'closed' statement. The open statement relates to the facts set out and agreed between the parties and the closed statement relates to their proposals for the future, which are only placed before a court after final agreement is reached. This would be made clear to, and agreed by, the parties before mediation began.

7.35 The Commission concluded that if one or both parties discloses information during mediation which could help to protect a child from harm this information should be passed to the relevant authorities - **that is, such information would not be treated as confidential.** However, **it would be subject to the statutory privilege,** and could not be admitted in evidence in any proceedings without the consent of both parties. This recommendation followed current practice at that time but now needs to be considered in the light of the 1993 Court of Appeal decision on *Re D (Minors) (Conciliation: Disclosure of Information)* [1993] 1 FCR 877, FD.

7.36 The general view of Consultees is that despite the decision in *Re D* there is a need for legislation to make the privilege rule clear. The Government, therefore, intends to legislate to provide for a statutory privilege as recommended by the Law Commission.

■ The role of the court in respect of mediated agreements

7.37 At present all District Judges examine consent ancillary relief applications, not only to ensure that the terms are correctly phrased and are within the powers of the court, but also to satisfy themselves of the overall fairness of the order in the light of the provisions of section 25 of the Matrimonial Causes Act 1973, and the information provided by the parties. Where one or both of the parties is acting in person and has not been legally advised, District Judges are also concerned to ensure that the party in person is fully informed and aware of the consequences of the order.

7.38 The Government proposes that the same procedural system should apply to mediated agreements. There was some support on consultation for a new system which would allow parties to register agreements with a court without the need for the court to consider them. While this has attractions, and would be entirely consistent with a system which encouraged 'private ordering' where appropriate, the Government believes that for the immediate future it would be desirable for mediated agreements to be subject to the same system as lawyer-negotiated agreements now are if couples want a court order. There would however **be no requirement that parties ask for their agreement to be approved as a court order unless they**

wished to do so. Many couples now enter into private agreements concerned with their decision to separate and/or divorce. There is no reason why couples should be deterred from taking this approach in the future if they wished.

Part C - Pilot Project

7.39 The Government's view is that an essential step in preparing for implementation of the proposals in this Paper will be a major comprehensive pilot project which will monitor and test the new arrangements, in so far as this is possible, before full implementation. There was strong support in the responses to the Consultation Paper for a project of this kind.

7.40 The Pilot will help the Legal Aid Board to develop auditable standards on which to base its Block Contract Specification for local mediation services. It will also focus on certain important aspects of the new process, including the extent to which couples seek to save their marriage; the information giving session; the use of an informational video (who and where); arrangements for the selection and training of mediators; the uptake of mediation and the number of mediators likely to be needed; the organization of and quality assurance procedures for the delivery of mediation services; the use of lawyers, and their educational and training needs and the allocation of legal aid.

7.41 This independently evaluated project will be designed in consultation with the Lord Chancellor's Department, which will also provide support for the project once in progress.

<table>
<tr><td>

**Chapter
8**

</td><td>

Extension of Proposals to Family Proceedings Other than Divorce

Availability of Mediation

</td></tr>
</table>

8.1 Although this White Paper has focused on the use of family mediation in the context of divorce proceedings, the advantages of family mediation are not confined to cases of this type. The Government believes that couples should be encouraged to consider using family mediation as a means of resolving issues in relation to children, the home and finance **whenever** this would be appropriate in a given case, and would be of benefit to the couple concerned. Family mediation may not be suitable in certain types of cases, or of benefit to certain couples. The Government believes, however, that family mediation should be available to couples who are involved in any type of family proceedings. Assistance should, however, be justified on the basis of an assessment of the means of the parties and the nature of the case.

The Information Session

8.2 It will take time for the necessary administrative arrangements relating to the information session to be put into place and become established. When the system for divorce proceedings is established, however, the Government will consider extending the requirement to attend an information session as a compulsory part of proceedings, to other appropriate cases, for example, disputes about residence of and contact with children.

Reform of Related Areas of Family Law and Procedures

Domestic Violence Remedies

9.1 The Family Homes and Domestic Violence Bill, currently before Parliament, clarifies and strengthens the civil remedies available for those who are in need of protection. The main object of this Bill is to provide a single consistent set of remedies which will be available in all courts with jurisdiction in family matters and to extend the categories of person who may apply for these remedies. The Bill introduces two types of order to replace the existing remedies, a non-molestation order to prohibit particular behaviour or 'molestation' in general, and an occupation order, with a variety of terms, including regulating and defining occupation rights in the home and the exclusion of the respondent from the home and, if necessary, a defined area around it.

9.2 When making an occupation order, the court can also:

➤ order either party to be granted the possession or use of the furniture, or other contents of the home; or

➤ impose obligations as to the repair and maintenance of the dwelling house, or obligations as to the payment of certain outgoings, for example, rent or mortgage payments.

9.3 The Bill also extends the court's existing power to transfer certain tenancies between spouses so as to enable orders to be made in respect of cohabitants as well as married couples. It allows cohabitants and former cohabitants to use the summary procedure under section 17 of the Married Women's Property Act 1882 and section 7 of the Matrimonial Causes (Property and Maintenance) Act 1958 to resolve property disputes. This procedure is at present only available to married or engaged couples.

Financial Provision Following Divorce

9.4 In addition to the major recommendations made concerning reform of the law of divorce, the Law Commission made minor recommendations in relation to the rules for variation of property and financial provision following divorce. The Government believes that the substantive law in this area should be examined as part of its programme for review of the family justice system. Such an examination will take place in due course. The Law Commission recommendations will be looked at in the context of that consideration.

Ancillary Relief Procedures

9.5 Procedures for Ancillary Relief are outside the scope of this White Paper. Many consultees, however, mentioned these matters. An informal group known as the Ancillary Relief Working Party has been looking at ways in which the process of Ancillary Relief might be reformed, and has made proposals for change. The Working Party consists of Family Division judges and representatives from the Family Law Bar Association, the Solicitors' Family Law Association and the Law Society. The Lord Chancellor's Department is working together with the Working Party in taking forward its proposals.

9.6 The Ancillary Relief Working Party's proposals are in the form of a draft rule and they seek to introduce a standard case-managed system for dealing with Ancillary Relief applications throughout the courts. The Lord Chancellor recently received views as part of a consultation on possible reform of this area. There remains, however, much work to be done before a decision can be made on the best option for reform.

Practice Direction by the President of the Family Division

9.7 The Government recognises that not all cases will be suitable for mediation, and that those cases which are not will either settle as a result of arms length negotiation through solicitors, or will be

adjudicated upon by the court. It is important that the conduct of ancillary relief proceedings should be efficient and effective, so that the matters at issue are resolved swiftly and cost effectively whether they are legally aided or not. **The Government welcomes the President's practice direction on case management, [1995] 1 All ER 586, FD, and hopes that this will result in a more efficient approach to the conduct of family cases.**

Lord Woolf's Review of Civil Court Procedures

9.8 The proposals in this Paper for the introduction of mediation, and the simplification of divorce procedures, together with the aims of the draft rule being considered by the Ancillary Relief Working Party, are all in keeping with the underlying philosophy of Lord Woolf's Review of Civil Court Procedures. This review aims at improving access to justice and to look at bringing civil court procedures under a single set of rules, so far as that is possible.

<table>
<tr><td>

**Chapter
10**

</td><td>

Conclusion

10.1 This White Paper sets out the Government's detailed proposals for reform of the divorce process in England and Wales. Divorce is an important and sensitive subject on which many people have strong views. The Government has therefore consulted widely and given serious thought to the options before coming to a final decision. The Government believes that the reforms now proposed in this White Paper represent the best means of achieving the Government's objectives. They will lead to a divorce process that:

</td></tr>
</table>

➤ supports the institution of marriage;

➤ helps to save marriages that can and should be saved;

➤ requires couples to consider carefully the consequences of divorce before taking any irreversible decisions;

➤ minimises bitterness and hostility and the trauma for children; and

➤ keeps to a minimum the cost of divorce to the parties and to the taxpayer.

10.2 The Government is committed to the view that a necessary step in preparing for the implementation of a new system is a comprehensive pilot project. The primary objective of such a project will be to ensure that the model for the delivery of information and mediation services, and the way in which allocation of state funding takes place, will support the principles of a good divorce process outlined above. In addition, it will determine mechanisms for quality assurance and ongoing evaluation of mediation services.

Summary of Consultation

Appendix A

Introduction

The Government's consultation on divorce law reform has involved three main parts:

➤ the Consultation Paper, published in December 1993 and titled *Looking to the Future - Mediation and the Ground for Divorce;*

➤ the Questionnaire, attached to the Summary of the Consultation Paper and sent out with copies of that Summary, and reproduced at Appendix B; and

➤ the MORI public opinion survey on attitudes to divorce law reform.

The response to the Consultation Paper has been largely qualitative and has come, in the main, from individuals and organisations with considerable experience in the field of family law and family breakdown. The detailed arguments and analyses presented by these consultees have been of immense value to the Government in its consideration of the case for reform.

The nature of the questionnaire was such that the types of results it produced were varied. Some of the questions were open ended, designed to elicit general comments from consultees. The remainder of the questions provided consultees with a variety of options, and asked them to select which they preferred. A number of consultees who filled out questionnaires also sent in full responses to the Consultation Paper. It was clear from the responses to the questionnaire that a large proportion came from persons with considerable personal or professional experience of divorce.

The survey carried out by MORI produced mainly numerical results. MORI interviewed two samples, one consisting of members of the general public (1,019 people), and one of divorced persons (527 people). In the following sections these groups are described as the general public sample, and the divorced sample respectively.

The results of consultation are presented under broad headings, taking each of the three strands of consultation in turn. The treatment of the material is dictated by the nature of the responses. Analysis is predominantly numerical in the sections dealing with MORI and parts of the questionnaire study, whereas the focus in the sections on the Consultation Paper is on the nature of the arguments put forward. Under each heading there is a section that presents the general balance of opinion on that issue.

PART A - CONSULTATION RESPONSES ON DIVORCE LAW AND PROCEDURES

Advantages and Disadvantages of the Current System

■ The consultation paper

Chapter 5 of the Consultation Paper put forward a number of criticisms of the current divorce system, and invited comments on these. The criticisms listed were:

➤ the present system allows divorce to be obtained quickly and easily without the parties being required to have regard to the consequences;

➤ the system does nothing to save the marriage;

➤ the system can make things worse for the children;

➤ the system is unjust and exacerbates bitterness and hostility;

➤ the system is confusing, misleading and open to abuse;

➤ the system is discriminatory; and

➤ the system distorts the parties bargaining positions.

◆ *The Present System Allows Divorce to be Obtained Quickly and Easily Without the Parties being Required to have Regard to the Consequences*

Consultees generally argued that it is an advantage that a quick divorce can be obtained. A quick divorce is not a disadvantage because:

➤ in situations of domestic violence women are in need of urgent relief; and

➤ spouses usually give a great deal of consideration before taking steps to break up a marriage.

Those who argued that the speed at which a divorce can be obtained is a disadvantage said that:

> it does not give enough time for the respondent spouse to consider his or her future; and

> spouses are rushed into divorce.

◆ *The System does nothing to Help Save the Marriage*

The response was virtually unanimous that the system is inimical to reconciliation. Reasons for this were that:

> any adversarial system is intrinsically likely to cause hostility;

> allegations of fault cause resentment; and

> the system does not provide any practical opportunity for counselling once the petition is filed.

◆ *The System can Make Things Worse for the Children*

Some consultees argued that the present system failed to ensure that adequate regard was paid to the interests of the children.

◆ *The System is Unjust and Exacerbates Bitterness and Hostility*

In general, consultees agreed that the system gave rise to a sense of injustice. In particular, three factors were emphasised. These were:

> the impracticality of defending behaviour petitions;

> the claim that 'blameless' spouses could be divorced against their will; and

> the claim that women do much better out of divorce than men.
There was virtually unanimous agreement that the system exacerbated hostility. Consultees' reasons were that:

> the system is adversarial;

> the system rewards allegations of fault; and

> no practical opportunities for marriage guidance or divorce counselling exist during the process.

♦ *The System is Confusing, Misleading and Open to Abuse*

Consultees agreed that the system was confusing and misleading. Consultees with an interest in the legal aspects of the process argued that the system was open to abuse because it encouraged petitioners to put forward bogus cases.

♦ *The System is Discriminatory*

This suggestion provoked little argument. Those who commented agreed that it was difficult for couples of limited means to rely on the separation facts, and that this represented an added incentive to allege fault.

♦ *The System Distorts the Parties' Bargaining Positions*

This suggestion did not provoke a great deal of comment. Comments were mainly made by interest groups or individuals with a specific concern in this area.

♦ *Other Aspects Raised*

Other criticisms included the failure of the courts to enforce contact orders, the substantial financial costs that could be incurred, especially in fees to solicitors and more generalised criticisms of the role of solicitors.

■ The questionnaire

Questions 1 to 3 of the questionnaire provided opportunities for consultees to express views on the advantages and disadvantages of the current system. Questions 1 and 2 were open ended, allowing consultees to comment freely. Question 3 listed a number of aspects of the divorce system, and asked consultees to comment on whether they thought the law should be changed with regard to each of these aspects.

◆ **Question 1 - Open Ended Comments on the Advantages of the Current System**

The most popular advantage mentioned in this section was the ability to obtain a divorce relatively quickly. Reasons given were as follows:

➤ a quick process is a relief to couples who have not taken the decision to divorce lightly; and

➤ speed is essential in domestic violence cases, or other intolerable situations.

A similar sentiment was expressed by consultees who saw the provision of a means of dissolving a broken marriage as a benefit in its own right.

Several consultees said that it was an advantage that divorce could be obtained without the need to allege fault, if one of the separation facts was relied upon. The special procedure, which allows a divorce to proceed without a detailed court enquiry into the breakdown of the marriage was also listed as an advantage by some consultees.

A variety of other advantages was mentioned. These included the one year bar, the accessibility of divorce (and legal aid), the cost, the provision of meaningful barriers to divorce which supports marriage and protects those who do not wish a divorce, the retention of some fault based facts, and the simplicity of the system.

◆ **Question 2 - Open Ended Comments about the Disadvantages of the Current System**

This question generated a great deal more comment than question 1. The content and the volume of the responses indicated that the majority of consultees agreed with the criticisms in Chapter 5 of the Consultation Paper.

The most frequently cited disadvantage was that the system exacerbates bitterness and hostility. Consultees mentioned the need to make allegations of fault in a system that is intrinsically adversarial and confrontational as the source of much hostility. A number considered that the system favours litigation and discourages reconciliation or mediation.

Several consultees thought that the current system allows divorce to be obtained too quickly or too easily. Reasons given included:

➤ easy/quick divorces devalue marriages;

➤ the system gives too little time for reflection; and

➤ there is little incentive for the parties to consider the consequences.

A number of consultees listed the more specific disadvantage that the ancillary matters (ie children and finance) were settled long after the decree absolute.

Several responses mentioned that the system does nothing to save marriages. Reasons given included the lack of opportunities to attempt reconciliation, and factors outside the ambit of divorce law, such as pre-marital education.

A number of responses demonstrated a clear sense of personal injustice, and claimed that the system contained a systematic bias against either men or women. Some responses argued that it was intrinsically unjust that someone could be divorced against their will.

Some consultees took the view that the divorce process sometimes causes harm and distress to children. One reason was that the process is 'adult focused', with children frequently being used as pawns in their parents' conflict. Other consultees stressed that the system does not give sufficient regard to the interests of children in matters that directly effect them, such as custody and access.

Several consultees said that the system was misleading and that the 'fact' relied upon in the divorce petition often bore no resemblance to the actual cause of the marriage breakdown.

A number of consultees agreed that the present system was confusing, not least because the ground for divorce is 'no fault' but three of the facts require evidence of fault. There was also agreement that the system/process was not only open to abuse, but that there was considerable abuse taking place. Several responses added that the divorce process encouraged parties to lie.

It was pointed out in a number of responses that the length of time required for the separation facts acted as an inducement for parties to use the fault-based facts. Some consultees argued that this represented a form of discrimination against couples who cannot afford to separate for two years without obtaining the divorce.

◆ Question Three

In this question, consultees were asked to select from a list which aspect(s) of the law and procedures relating to dissolution of marriage should be changed. The breakdown of responses indicates consultees views about the relative advantages and disadvantages of the current system.

There was support for change in respect of each of the aspects listed, and in most cases this support was very considerable. Strongest support was expressed for reform that would lead to couples being more aware of the consequences of divorce (85%), and to a reduction in hostility between the partners (85%). Over 70% of consultees also supported reform that would make the system clearer in purpose and more straightforward in practice (80%), better at saving saveable marriages (77%) and better able to give consideration to the children involved (71%). The least support was shown for making the system better at establishing the innocence and blameworthiness of each party.

■ MORI opinion poll

The majority of the general public sample (72%) and the divorced sample (79%) agreed that the law should not force those who wish to divorce quickly to make accusations of adultery or intolerable behaviour. By contrast, the majority in both samples (65% and 77% respectively) also agreed that the law should allow one person a divorce immediately if the other person has behaved intolerably or committed adultery.

These results appear contradictory until interpreted in the light of qualitative data reported by MORI. Opinion seems to be that while a person may privately decide to divorce on the basis of adultery or intolerable behaviour, the requirement that these faults be listed publicly as part of the divorce process is wrong. This interpretation is borne out by the net agreement in both samples (+8% and +22% respectively) that anyone who wants a divorce should be able to get one.

■ Summary of consultation on the advantages and disadvantages of the current system

It was clear from all strands of the consultation that the current system is perceived to have more faults than virtues. In general, the criticisms listed in Chapter 5 of the Consultation Paper were seen as the main flaws, with particular emphasis on the failure of the system to help save marriages that can and should be saved, and to minimise hostility and bitterness between the parties.

The results of consultation departed from the Paper in one main regard - the speed and ease with which it is possible to obtain a divorce. There was a general view, particularly among those with personal or professional experience of divorce, that in many circumstances it is an advantage that divorce can be obtained quickly and easily. The responses did, however, indicate agreement with the Government's view that the system should do more to encourage divorcing couples to consider the consequences of divorce. It was considered by some to be a significant disadvantage that matters to do with children and finance are frequently not addressed until after the divorce process is complete.

The Case for Reform

■ The consultation paper

Not surprisingly in view of the preceding discussion, most consultees considered there was a case for reform. The most cited three reasons in support of reform were as follows:

➤ the hostility between the parties caused by the adversarial process and the fault-based facts;

➤ the injustice of the present system, since there is no realistic opportunity to answer allegations of fault, and there is a bias in favour of men/women; and

➤ the fact that the present system allows *de facto* divorce on demand.

A minority of consultees did not consider there was a need for fundamental reform.

■ The questionnaire

The majority of consultees agreed that fundamental changes were required to the present system:

➤ to minimise bitterness;

➤ to remove injustice, particularly the fact that the respondent had no realistic opportunity to answer allegations of fault in the petition; and

➤ to enable parties to take greater responsibility for making arrangements for the future.

■ Summary of consultation on the need for reform

It was clear that the weight of opinion across the consultation was in favour of change. Different consultees stressed different motivations for reform, but the general tone was in favour of reforms that would reduce the bitterness and hostility currently attendant on the process.

Objectives for Divorce Law and Procedures

In Chapters 1 and 4 of the Consultation Paper the Government's objectives for the law and procedures surrounding the dissolution of marriage were set out. These were:

➤ to support the institution of marriage;

➤ to include practicable steps to prevent the irretrievable breakdown of marriages;

➤ to ensure that the parties understand the practical consequences of divorce before taking any irreversible decision;

➤ where divorce is unavoidable, to minimise the bitterness and hostility between the parties and reduce the trauma for the children; and

➤ to keep to the minimum the cost to the parties and the taxpayer.

These objectives attracted comment from those who made full responses to the Consultation Paper.

■ The consultation paper

Most consultees agreed that a divorce process should embody the first four objectives, although some were sceptical that reconciliation was possible once a petition was filed.

Some consultees contrasted the Consultation Paper's objectives with the 1966 Law Commission report entitled *The Field of Choice.* They and others were concerned that 'justice' was not an objective of the divorce process as it was in 1966. No response contained any attempt to define what constituted 'justice'.

Some consultees considered that the objectives did not give sufficient weighting to the interests of the children of the marriage. In particular, a few argued that the interests of children required there to be a prohibition on divorce where there were children under a certain age.

■ Summary of consultation on objectives for reform

There was general agreement with the Government's stated objectives. Some consultees, however, wished to see certain aspects strengthened.

Options for Change

■ The consultation paper

In Chapter 6 of the Consultation Paper several options for reform of divorce law were presented. Comment on these options is discussed under the following headings:

> the ground for divorce and the method of proof;

> the length of the period for consideration and reflection;

> the hardship bar;

> judicial separation; and

> nullity.

◆ *The Ground for Divorce and the Method of Proof*

Consultees were in broad agreement that the ground for divorce should remain the irretrievable breakdown of the marriage. There was, however, disagreement about the method by which such a breakdown should be demonstrated. In general, consultation supported one of the two following options:

> the breakdown of the marriage should be proved by the sole fact of a period for consideration and reflection (Option A); or

> the breakdown of the marriage should be capable of establishment by more than one method, in a 'mixed system' which would include both fault-based and no fault facts (Option B).

Option A was supported in the majority of responses to the Consultation Paper made by professionals and their representative organisations. The reasons consultees gave in favour of the period for consideration and reflection were the same as listed in the Consultation Paper. The principal advantages were perceived to be that:

> it was a no fault fact and therefore avoided the injustice, bitterness and resentment that arose when petitions were based on allegations of fault;

> the passage of time would act as a brake on hasty applications and would enable the parties to seek marriage guidance; and

> the parties would be required to think about and make arrangements for their lives post divorce before the divorce was granted.

Option B would be based upon the present system with some substantive change. Some consultees favoured a reduction in the separation periods and some argued that there should be a fact of mutual consent. This option had the support of a minority of professional consultees. The reasons given in favour of this option were that:

➤ fault-based divorce enables a party to get a quick divorce in cases of domestic violence;

➤ fault-based divorce provides a moral basis for conduct within marriage;

➤ fault-based divorce ensures that innocent spouses cannot be unilaterally divorced in a short period of time;

➤ it is just that a party who has caused the breakdown of the marriage by misconduct should be held responsible by the court; and

➤ those who wish to divorce consensually can do so without allegations of misconduct.

◆ ***The Length of the Period for Consideration and Reflection***

Support was clear for a new system in which the ground for divorce remained the irretrievable breakdown of the marriage, but the method of proof was changed to a period for consideration and reflection. Those who favoured this option generally suggested a period of 12 months. The reasons given were:

➤ a fixed period is a practical necessity;

➤ 12 months is a reasonable time in most cases for parties to come to terms with their situation; and

➤ 12 months is long enough for completion of the arrangements for living apart.

Support for a longer or a shorter period was limited to a small number of responses.

In the Consultation Paper the possibility that the length of the period might be different depending on whether there were children was put forward. There was no support for this proposal because:

➤ children would suffer where parents wanting a divorce blamed their children for any delay; and

➤ it would harm the children.

The Consultation Paper also discussed the possibility that the court might have a power to abridge the period for consideration and reflection. Consultees were evenly divided on this point. Reasons against a power of abridgement included:

➤ it would weaken the principle of a single period for consideration and reflection, the principle being that irretrievable breakdown is established only by the lapse of the period of time;

➤ issues of domestic violence should be dealt with outside the divorce process;

➤ such a power would be abused and in time would become a standard route for a quick divorce;

➤ a power of abridgment would lead to litigation, uncertainty and acrimony all of which increase costs; and

➤ such a power would be unfair on the non-applicant spouse.

Reasons given in favour of a power of abridgment were as follows:

➤ the problems of housing: in domestic violence cases, remedies for occupation of the family home are inadequate;

➤ such a power could be exercised when the ancillaries have been agreed. At this point the period for consideration and reflection no longer serves any useful purpose; and

➤ in exceptional circumstances there should be a power of abridgment to deal with hard cases. (In many instances exceptional circumstances were not defined.)

The Consultation Paper also suggested that the court might be given a power to extend the period in some circumstances. The response was on balance in favour of the court having a power to extend the period and/or completion of the ancillaries being a condition precedent of the divorce order, because it is desirable that the ancillaries should be settled before the marriage is dissolved and there will be cases where the ancillaries will not be agreed at the end of the 12 month period.

A minority were opposed to the power to extend for the following reasons:

> it would prejudice the interests of children. Their interests are best served by a system embodying finality and certainty; and

> it would lead to increased litigation.

◆ **The Hardship Bar**

The majority were in favour of the retention of the hardship bar for the following reasons:

> it provides a safeguard for an elderly wife whose husband lacks the resources necessary to compensate her for loss of a contingent widow's pension; and

> in some communities divorce can cause hardship irrespective of its financial consequences eg Jewish and ethnic minority communities.

The minority were opposed to retention for the following reasons:

> it is anachronistic; and

> the solution to the problem is reform of the law on pensions.

◆ **Judicial Separation**

The overwhelming majority of consultees were in favour of retaining judicial separation for the following reasons:

> it is a valuable alternative remedy where the parties have religious or conscientious objections to divorce;

➤ it is valuable where it is necessary to start proceedings within the first year of marriage; and

➤ it is a useful remedy to preserve contingent pension rights.

◆ *Nullity*

Consultees argued that discussion or reform of this issue was not necessary or appropriate in the context of divorce. Further, a more in depth examination needed to take place.

■ The questionnaire

Questions 4 to 16 of the questionnaire dealt with the options for reform. Questions 4 to 7 dealt with the ground for divorce and the method of proof. Questions 8 to 13 dealt with the length of the period. Questions 15 and 16 covered judicial separation.

◆ *Questions 4 to 7 - The Ground for Divorce and the Method of Proof*

Consultees were presented with a list of options for the ground for divorce. They were asked to circle one option as their preference (question 4) and any of the remaining options that they thought were valid (question 5).

Divorce after a period for consideration and reflection was by a very large margin the most popular option as a single preference (62%). No other option was selected by more than 9% of consultees. When asked to circle alternatives that they considered to be valid, consultees favoured alternative no fault grounds such as mutual consent (59%) and separation (54%).

Those who favoured separation as the sole ground for divorce predominantly suggested a separation of one year, and did not consider that the consent of both parties should be required for divorce in these circumstances.

◆ *Questions 8 to 12 - The Length of the Period for Consideration and Reflection*

Consultees who selected divorce after a period for consideration and reflection as their preference were asked to comment on how long the period should be. The single most popular option was 12 months (57%), followed by 6 months (27%). No other length of time was favoured by more than 7% of consultees. The majority (66%) thought the period should be the same for everyone, regardless of whether they had children.

Question 10 asked consultees to comment on whether there should be a power for the period to be reduced in individual cases. Consultees considered that the desirability of such a power would depend on what the normal length of the period was. If the period were 6 months, there should be no power to shorten it. If the period were 18 months or longer there should be a power to abridge. Consultees were divided as to whether a period of 12 months should be capable of abridgement. By contrast, the majority of consultees saw the main rationale for a power of abridgement as being the reduction of suffering for the children.

Question 12 asked consultees what circumstances would justify an extension of the period. Again, the welfare of the children was seen as the main justification, with arrangements for financial provision also mentioned by a majority of consultees.

Finally, consultees were asked to say what matters should be finalised as a pre-condition of the granting of a divorce decree. A clear majority (80%) favoured making the arrangement for children a pre-condition of divorce, while slim majorities also favoured finalisation of financial (56%) and property/accommodation (55%) arrangements.

■ The MORI Poll

◆ *The Ground for Divorce and the Method of Proof*

The MORI Poll presented people with a list of grounds for divorce, and asked them to select which would be their first and second choices to be the sole method of obtaining a divorce. In both samples divorce after a fixed period for reflection and consideration was the single most popular choice, followed by divorce by mutual consent.

The MORI Poll also asked people to select which grounds for divorce they would find unacceptable. The single most popular option, by a considerable margin, was divorce on demand by one partner without having to give a reason.

◆ **The Length of the Period for Consideration and Reflection**

The majority of people in both samples said that they favoured a change in the law so that divorce would be obtained only on the basis of a period of consideration and reflection (69% general public; 66% divorced). These people were asked what the length of the period should be. Most people selected a period up to and including two years, with the most popular range being 13-24 months in the general public sample, and 7-12 months in the divorced sample.

People were also asked whether the period should be longer or shorter for couples with children. In both groups the most popular option was for the period to be the same (49% general public; 58% divorced) while a longer period was favoured by 36% of the general public sample and 26% of the divorced sample.

People were presented with a long list of additional reasons why the period of time might be lengthened or shortened. Only three of these received the support of more than 7% of either sample. They were:

➤ to make arrangements for the children (30% general public; 16% divorced);

➤ to get away from an abusive spouse (13% general public; 15% divorced); and

➤ to make financial arrangements (11% general public; 12% divorced).

On the question of whether the courts should have the power to extend the period in individual cases there was a clear difference between the two groups. A majority in the general public sample said

that the courts should have this power (56%), while in the divorced sample opinion was divided between those who favoured such a power (41%) and those who opposed it (47%).

■ Summary of Consultation on Options for Reform

In all three strands of the consultation there was clear support for the option of divorce on the ground of irretrievable breakdown of the marriage, as demonstrated by a period for consideration and reflection. Responses to the Consultation Paper, the questionnaire and the divorced sample in the MORI Poll were predominantly in favour of the Law Commission recommendation that the period should be 12 months. The general public sample in the MORI Poll preferred a longer period.

Support for abridgement depended on the length of the period - the longer the period the more necessary it would be to have a power of abridgement. Support for a power to extend the period was less equivocal, with all strands of the consultation indicating some support for such a power in order to ensure that as often as possible all the necessary arrangements were complete before the divorce decree was granted.

Consultees strongly favoured retention of the decree of judicial separation, bringing the procedures into line with any reform of the divorce law. The retention of the hardship bar was also favoured. It was generally thought that the law of nullity was outside the scope of the present consideration of reform.

Divorce Procedures

The bulk of responses on questions of divorce procedures came from the Consultation Paper. The questionnaire posed two questions about the role of the court. MORI did not assess public opinion about divorce procedures.

■ The Consultation Paper

◆ *Initial Documentation*

The majority of those who commented on this took the view that the initiating document should be non-adversarial. The contents should be as brief as possible.

◆ *Accompanying Documents*

Most consultees who expressed a view said that the initiating document should be accompanied by a statement containing details about the children. The statement should focus on facts rather than proposals because:

> ➤ the filing of proposals for the care of the children might often lead to allegations of fault being imported into the divorce process, leading to an increase in tension and bitterness;

> ➤ the spouses might not, at the time of filing the statement of breakdown, have had the opportunity to discuss any proposals;

> ➤ such proposals filed at this stage would, in any event, be based on incomplete information.

There was no consensus on whether parties should be required to provide information about property and finance.

◆ *Role of the Court*

There was broad agreement that the court should perform a 'checking' role in monitoring the progress of cases because:

> ➤ the court should, in general, have more control over the proceedings;

> ➤ it would enable the court to check that parties have understood the purpose of the period for consideration and reflection; and

> ➤ the court would be able to ascertain whether there was a need for orders or directions.

Consultees did not address the issue of whether the supervisory role of the court was simply to manage the case, or to make substantive orders on its own motion.

Opinion was split between those who favoured the court carrying out 'paper' assessments, and those who preferred supervision to take the form of a judicial hearing. Supporters of the latter argued that it would impress upon the parties the importance of the need for consideration and reflection, and to make proper arrangements. Those who preferred a paper assessment said that the court could supervise the progress of proceedings as effectively without court hearings.

The majority who commented considered that the checking role should be exercised within the first 12 weeks of the process. Some, however, favoured 16 weeks or 6 months.

◆ Inquisitorial Jurisdiction

The overwhelming majority of consultees considered it essential for the court to check draft consent orders for jurisdiction and enforceability. The reason given was that orders are often technically defective. Nearly all consultees thought that this checking role should apply equally to mediated agreements.

Professional opinion was, on balance, in favour of the court retaining an inquisitorial jurisdiction over consent orders and mediators but some responses were opposed.

◆ Which Court?

The majority of consultees were opposed to divorce proceedings being commenced in the Family Proceedings Court (FPC) because:

> the FPC does not have the necessary facilities and expertise for handling complex technical paperwork; and

> proceedings initiated in the FPC which led to any complex ancillaries would have to be transferred at some stage to a divorce county court. This would be expensive and unnecessarily complicated.

◆ *The Divorce Process and Domestic Violence*

Most consultees supported the proposal that remedies for domestic violence should remain outside the divorce process.

■ The questionnaire

The questionnaire asked consultees to say whether they thought the court should have a role in checking the arrangements for children, property and finance both during and at the end of the process of divorce. There was majority support for such a role during the process (63%) and at the end (73%).

■ Summary of consultation on divorce procedures

Responses in both strands of the consultation that addressed divorce procedures favoured procedures that reflected the objectives of minimising hostility and bitterness. There was broad support for the court taking a more active role in the process, supervising in general, and making directions in cases where there was perceived to be a need for such intervention. Consultees took the view that divorce should remain in the divorce county court.

PART B - CONSULTATION RESPONSES ON FAMILY MEDIATION

The Usefulness of Family Mediation

■ The Consultation Paper

In the Consultation Paper the principles and objectives of family mediation were set out. Consultees were asked the following questions:

➤ do the advantages claimed for mediation outweigh the disadvantages to the extent that mediation should be built into a reformed system of divorce;

➤ are there particular steps that could be taken to maximise the effect of the advantages in personal and economic terms for the separating couple and their children; and

➤ is there a case for making mediation a compulsory step in the divorce process?

◆ *Advantages and Disadvantages*

In general, consultees agreed that the advantages of mediation outweighed its disadvantages. Advantages emphasised included most of those listed in the Consultation Paper. On the side of caution, two arguments were particularly mentioned. They were:

➤ family mediation might not bring about financial savings on the scale that the Consultation Paper envisages because of the need for legal advice to take place alongside the mediation process; and

➤ there remains a lack of evidence about the effectiveness of family mediation.

◆ *Maximising the Advantages*

Many consultees saw the organisation of mediation as the key to its success. Most opposed the suggestion that a new body should be set up to run family mediation, and favoured instead the notion that existing services should be built on wherever possible.

Consultees also emphasised that, in order to be successful, mediation services had to be available. This included good geographical coverage, and short intervals between referral and first appointment.

A number of consultees took the view that access to independent legal advice throughout the mediation process was a key to its success. This point was particularly emphasised in relation to mediation of all issues, that is, comprehensive mediation.

Other relevant points put forward included the consideration of ethnic minorities, the involvement of children, simplified court procedures and powers for judges to direct couples to mediation.

◆ *Compulsory Mediation?*

Consultees were completely opposed to mandatory mediation. Instead, the discussion was predominantly focused on how to encourage parties to try mediation without compelling them to do so. An increase in the power of the court was favoured, whereas the suggestion that the grant of legal aid might be contingent on willingness to try mediation was opposed.

■ The questionnaire

Three questions were posed about family mediation in general. The first asked:

> ➤ taking into account the various advantages and disadvantages claimed for mediation, do you think it should be introduced within a reformed system of divorce or kept separate?

A large majority of consultees (70%) answered 'Yes, Introduced'. Those who did so were asked the second two questions. The first of these provided space for consultees to write in their answers, and asked:

> ➤ in what ways, if any, can mediation be used to maximise the personal and economic well-being of the separating couple and their children?

Consultees focused in their responses on the twin themes of adequate funding and the requirement for access to independent legal advice alongside the mediation process. Finally, consultees were asked:

> ➤ is there a case for making mediation a compulsory step in the divorce process?

A large majority of consultees (69%) answered 'yes' to this question.

Question 28, which asked for additional comments on the proposals in the summary of the Consultation Paper, also attracted responses on the topic of family mediation. Some consultees reiterated the advantages of family mediation in reducing conflict, encouraging careful thought, and making proper arrangements, especially with regard to children. A few consultees expressed caution about the cost-

effectiveness of family mediation in this section. Responses in this section also contradicted the majority judgement on the question of making mediation compulsory. Those who commented on this issue opposed the idea, and some described it as a contradiction in terms.

■ MORI Survey

Public awareness of mediation services was found to be very low. Over half of consultees said that they had never heard of family mediation. Fewer than 10% said that they knew more than a little about family mediation. Ignorance was the main reason for not using mediation: the majority on the general public sample said they would not use family mediation because they knew nothing about it (62%), but the proportion was lower among divorced people, where 23% attributed the fact that they had not used mediation to ignorance. Three people had experience of mediation and were broadly positive, listing the reduced need for lawyers' help as the most important benefit.

When mediation was explained to them, over 80% of consultees in both samples said it would be very useful or fairly useful. When asked why, the four most important advantages listed by divorced people were:

➤ the involvement of a neutral third party (26%);

➤ a more amicable and less argumentative approach (24%);

➤ the opportunity to focus on the children (24%); and

➤ the possibility for honest exchange of views (23%).

Divorced peoples' reasons for saying that mediation would **not** be useful included:

➤ when people seek divorce the situation has gone too far (22%);

➤ the partner is too unreasonable (19%); and

➤ once one has decided to divorce it is all over (15%).

This indicates that many who said mediation would not be useful misunderstood its nature and purpose.

The MORI survey asked consultees to say how strongly they agreed that divorcing couples should be required to make arrangements for living separately **before** the divorce is finalised. An extraordinary majority of divorced consultees agreed (92%), most of them strongly (59%). As a follow up question, consultees were asked to say what the best means of coming to such arrangements would be. There was a clear preference among divorced people and the general public for settling matters out of court.

■ Summary of consultation on the usefulness of family mediation

Responses in all strands of the consultation showed support for the principles and objectives of family mediation. Consultees echoed the advantages listed in the Consultation Paper, and argued in support of an increased use of mediation by couples going through separation and divorce.

Responses from the general public indicated a low level of awareness of the nature and aims of mediation, especially in the MORI poll. When explained, family mediation was perceived as attractive and likely to be useful.

Caution was expressed on two fronts, that is, the costs of mediation and the lack of research into its effectiveness. Consultees emphasised the need for mediation to take place alongside independent legal advice.

Integration of Mediation into the Divorce Process

■ The Consultation Paper

The Consultation Paper suggested a number of ways in which mediation might be integrated into the reformed process of obtaining a divorce. One of the main suggestions was that all those wishing to initiate the process should be required to attend an initial interview, at which the nature of divorce and the principles and objectives of family mediation would be explained. Consultees were asked:

➤ should there be a single first port of call for everyone wishing to initiate the divorce process, and should it involve a personal interview;

➤ would such a personal interview be likely to encourage couples to mediate, at least in the first instance;

➤ who should conduct such interviews;

➤ what information should be included in the initial interview, and in what form; and

➤ should the courts be responsible for ensuring that draft consent orders were within statutory powers and were enforceable?

◆ *A Single First Port of Call?*

Consultees' views on the desirability of an initial interview depended on what they understood to be its purpose - there was not a uniform interpretation of the Government's Consultation Paper proposal. Broadly speaking, however, support for additional information giving facilities was widespread, and those who saw this facility as moving beyond the simplest information giving function agreed that it would need to involve a personal interview. Some consultees suggested that more than one interview might be necessary.

Support for the Government's suggestion that the initial interview might represent the necessary first step in initiating the divorce process was less substantial. The principal argument against this suggestion was that for many if not most spouses the natural first port of call was a solicitor's office. There was thus a risk of duplication.

◆ *Would it Encourage Couples to Mediate?*

The response of consultees to the Consultation Paper on this question was simple. A single first port of call interview would probably encourage couples to go to mediation (but this might not always be a good thing). It was not possible to say how significant this impact would be - it would depend in large part on whether there were adequate and competent mediation services available.

◆ *What Information Should be Included?*

A number of consultees emphasised that, in addition to the Government's suggestions, information might need to be provided on agencies able to provide services for children, and about the possible impact of the Child Support Agency on any arrangements that were made in mediation or solicitor-led negotiations. In this connection, the provision of information relevant to victims of domestic violence was also emphasised.

Consultees were given pause by the suggestion that the initial interview might give legal information. The substantive objection was to interviewers giving legal **advice**, but it was noted that the distinction between legal information and legal advice is in practice tricky to draw. Even if this was successfully drawn, the amount of relevant legal information needed would require the interviewer to possess a very significant knowledge of family law, which might not be possessed by someone lacking a legal qualification.

Some consultees opposed the initial interviewer giving information on costs, on the grounds that clients might be induced on this basis to make an inappropriate decision about which services to seek. The counter-argument was also made, however, that clients will insist on being able to take cost considerations into account when deciding on the best course of action.

Many consultees emphasised the need for objectivity in the information provided, and the need for it to attempt to overcome communication difficulties.

◆ *Who Should Conduct It?*

There was no support for the setting up of a new independent organisation. Reasons given included the tinge of additional bureaucracy, the expense, the failure to make use of existing skills and services, the option of creating an 'umbrella' to control standards if uniformity was required, and the intrinsic impossibility of obtaining the coverage necessary. Thus, views were essentially divided between the options of using court welfare staff, and local mediation services, with some other suggestions also being put forward.

The arguments against the court welfare services being used had to do with 'court phobia', that is, the sense that having to attend an interview at court might put people off. The arguments against using existing local mediation services had largely to do with the danger of conflicts of interest.

Consultees were particularly concerned to comment on the range and standard of skills that the initial interviewer required, and on whether the responsibility for allocating public funds should rest with the interviewer.

There was a consensus that if the role of the initial interviewer were to extend beyond the most rudimentary information giving, there would be a need for that person to possess a wide range of skills. Consultees agreed that a considerable knowledge of the law relating to divorce would be required, and some insisted that this should consist in a professional legal qualification. Consultees also pointed out that the interviewer would require good inter-personal skills.

Consultees were mostly hostile to the suggestion that the initial interviewer might have responsibility for the allocation of public funds, although most saw the benefit in the interviewer being able to make some assessment of means. The arguments were twofold: there is already a tried and tested machinery for assessing eligibility for legal aid, handling appeals, and making payment; and responsibility for public funds would threaten the perceived and actual neutrality of the interviewer.

◆ *Should the Courts Check Draft Consent Orders?*

The overwhelming majority of consultees considered that it was essential for the court to continue to check draft consent orders for jurisdiction and enforceability.

Consultees also commented on whether the court ought to play some role in ensuring that the orders were 'fair'. Most were opposed, or else emphasised the need for additional judicial resources in order to achieve this. Consultees also wondered whether there was always a need for orders to be made when agreements had been reached between private individuals about private matters.

■ The Questionnaire

Four questions were posed about the initial interview proposals. Firstly, consultees were asked to say whether they thought there should be a single first port of call for anyone wishing to initiate the divorce process, and whether it should involve a personal interview. The majority (68%) thought that there should be an initial first port of call interview, and that it should involve a personal interview. Only a few thought there should be no first port of call (18%) or that there should be one but without an interview (7%).

Some consultees' commented on the initial interview proposals under Question 28. These comments confirmed the general encouragement, but with some reservations. Once again, the need for the service to be properly funded, and not to exclude access to legal advice was emphasised. Several consultees questioned how realistic the objective of a joint interview would be, but emphasised that both partners must attend at some point in order for the purpose of the interview to be met. Several consultees also questioned the advisability of making the interview compulsory.

Question 23 offered consultees the opportunity to circle as many of a list of possible types of information to be provided by the initial interview as they wished. All the information types were popular, with over 75% of consultees circling each of the five possibilities. The rank ordering was as follows:

➤ information about mediation (95%);

➤ information about marriage guidance (93%);

➤ information about divorce law (86%);

➤ information about the procedure for getting divorced (83%); and

➤ information on welfare and tax matters (78%).

Few consultees (27%) took the opportunity to suggest additional types of information that the initial interview might provide.

Finally, consultees were asked to state their preferred option as to how the information should be presented. The majority (75%) said that there should be a single information pack, with 44% in favour of a video and 38% saying that leaflets would be a good option.

As was stated in the section on divorce procedures, a majority (63%) of consultees to the questionnaire thought that the court should verify the arrangements that a couple were making for a life apart. A larger majority (73%) thought that the court should approve the final arrangements.

Some clearly favoured an increase in the powers and role of the court to supervise the process - ensuring fairness as well as legality and enforceability, and giving directions concerning the services that couples should seek. Others saw problems with an increased role for the court, on a variety of grounds ranging from principle to practicality.

■ Summary of the Consultation on Integration of Mediation into the Divorce Process

There was general recognition that awareness of the nature of divorce and of the support services available to divorcing couples is very low. Most consultees supported the idea of making attendance at an information giving interview a necessary part of the divorce process. The principal reservations expressed about this proposal were in connection with the nature of the legal input that might take place at this interview. Most thought there should be no legal advice given.

Consultees thought that existing services should be the basis for deciding who should conduct the interview. Most favoured a role for the court in checking agreements reached in mediation, and there was some support for making it possible for couples who wished to do so to obtain legal advice from the same solicitor in connection with individual aspects of their case.

Public Funding of Family Mediation

■ The Consultation Paper

The Consultation Paper suggested that the Government might make public funds available to help meet the costs of family mediation for couples or individuals of limited means. Consultees were asked:

➤ are the Government's intended criteria appropriate for determining who should receive public assistance in future with the costs of mediation and legal advice on separation and divorce;

➤ should it be possible for a divorcing couple who have mediated issues in dispute to obtain advice from the same solicitor;

➤ would immediately enforceable costs orders offer a fair way of preventing an uncooperative spouse from behaving unreasonably;

➤ what arrangements should be made for the review of the decisions of the interviewer about publicly funded assistance;

◆ *Eligibility Criteria*

Consultees had little difficulty accepting that state funding of mediation services should be subject to similar criteria to those that apply for legal aid. Consultees did, however, foresee specific problems with the criterion of reasonableness. In particular, consultees emphasised the following points:

➤ a refusal to accept mediation should not be automatically determined as unreasonable; and

➤ neither mediators nor initial interviewers should be responsible for withholding public funds on these grounds (most favoured the 'fund-holder' playing this role).

Consultees saw few problems, however, with the initial interviewer making a preliminary means assessment.

Consultees also commented on the role of the statutory charge in relation to mediation costs. Generally, responses showed that there were arguments both in favour of disapplying the statutory charge, and also against doing so. Disapplying the charge would encourage mediation, but would also run contrary to the notion of placing publicly funded clients in the same position as privately paying persons.

◆ *Advice from the Same Solicitor*

This question did not receive a great deal of comment from consultees outside the practising profession(s). Opinion fell into three groups:

➤ those who opposed the notion on principled grounds;

➤ those who reluctantly accepted the principle, but thought that in practice there would be almost no cases in which the absence of a conflict of interest could be guaranteed; and

➤ those who accepted the principle and thought that it would be applicable in some or many cases.

◆ *Immediately Enforceable Costs Orders*

In consultees' opinions, the making of immediately enforceable costs orders should remain the function of the court, and of the court only. The frequency with which consultees made this point seemed to result from a misunderstanding that powers to make such costs orders might be extended. In addition, however, there was much doubt about the current effectiveness of such orders. Consultees wish to see the court playing a more active role in using its powers to make orders, and ensuring that the orders were enforced.

◆ *Arrangements for Review of Decisions about Publicly Funded Assistance?*

Most consultees opposed the notion that the initial interviewer should have any responsibility for allocating public funds. Consultees, however, took the view that, if this option was ignored, the Legal Aid Board's machinery might be used, and if not, something similar.

■ The questionnaire

Consultees who completed the questionnaire were invited to say whether they agreed or disagreed with the statement that where a couple had mediated issues in dispute it should be possible for them to obtain advice from the same solicitor. A slight majority (51%) agreed with this statement, while 40% disagreed and the remainder did not know.

Consultees who commented further on this proposal were alarmed, and emphasised again the need for independent legal advice. It is not clear to what extent these consultees properly understood that the suggestion was to allow advice from the same solicitor as an option to couples who had made all their arrangements through mediation.

■ Summary of consultation on public funding for family mediation

There was general support for making the criteria for eligibility the same as those that apply in legal aid, and some support for allowing couples to see the same solicitor in certain circumstances. A general concern was expressed that access to legal advice should not be limited on the basis of participation or refusal to participate in mediation.

Questionnaire attached to the summary of the consultation paper

Appendix B

JN/7953
(1-4)

Serial No . . . .
(5-8)

Thank you for your help in taking part in this consultation exercise about family mediation and divorce. The Government has issued a consultation paper and a summary on which this questionnaire is based. Your replies will reflect your views most accurately if you answer strictly in the order in which they are presented.

Where appropriate, please ring your preferred answer.

| DIVORCE |

Q1 Overall, what in your opinion, are the <u>main</u> advantages of the present system of divorce law and procedure in England and Wales? PLEASE WRITE IN

. . . . (9)

. . . . (10)

. . . .

Q2 And, what in your opinion, are the <u>main</u> disadvantages of the present system of divorce law and procedure? PLEASE WRITE IN

. . . . (11)

. . . . (12)

. . . .

Q3 From the following list of aspects of dissolution of marriage, can you tell me whether or not you think the law and procedures relating to each should be changed?
PLEASE CIRCLE ONE ANSWER FOR EACH AT A-I

		Should be	Should not be	Don't know	
A	The time it takes to obtain a divorce	1	2	3	13
B	Divorcing couples being made aware of the consequences of divorce	1	2	3	14
C	Rescuing 'saveable' marriages	1	2	3	15
D	The consideration given to children of divorcing couples	1	2	3	16
E	Attempting to ensure that justice is done regarding the extent of each party's innocence or blameworthiness	1	2	3	17
F	Minimising hostility between partners	1	2	3	18
G	Being clear in purpose and straightforward in practice	1	2	3	19
H	Some petitioners or respondents being placed in a stronger bargaining position than their partner in the divorce process	1	2	3	20
I	Other aspects which may need changing (PLEASE WRITE IN)	1	2	3	21

. . . .

Q4 **Which, if any, of the following is your preferred option for the basis for divorce?** PLEASE CIRCLE ONE ANSWER AT Q4 BELOW

Q5 **And which others are valid?** PLEASE CIRCLE AS MANY AS APPLY AT Q5 BELOW

	Q4	Q5
Divorce based on fault or blame	1	1
Divorce after a period for consideration and reflection	2	2
Immediate unilateral demand	3	3
Mutual consent	4	4
Separation	5	5
Inquiry into marriage breakdown	6	6
Other basis (PLEASE WRITE IN)	7	7
....		
None	8	8
Don't know	9	9

22/23

PLEASE ANSWER Q6-Q7 IF SEPARATION IS YOUR PREFERRED OPTION

Q6 **How long a period of separation do you think is appropriate to be grounds for divorce?** PLEASE CIRCLE ONE ANSWER AT Q6 BELOW

One year	1
Two years	2
Three years	3
Four years	4
Five years	5
Other (PLEASE SPECIFY)	6

24

....

Q7 **Should the consent of both parties be required for divorce on the grounds of separation?** PLEASE CIRCLE ONE ANSWER AT Q7 BELOW

Yes	1
No	2

25

Q8 ANSWER Q8-Q12 IF YOU SAID YOUR PREFERRED OPTION IS DIVORCE AFTER A PERIOD FOR CONSIDERATION AND REFLECTION.

How long do you think the <u>minimum basic period</u> for consideration should be? PLEASE CIRCLE ONE ANSWER AT Q8 BELOW

Six months	1
12 months	2
18 months	3
24 months	4
More than 24 months	5
Don't know	6

26

Q9 **And should there be a longer period for those with children or not? If so, how long should the extra period be?** PLEASE CIRCLE ONE ANSWER AT Q9 BELOW

No	1
Yes:	
One month	2
Three months	3
More than three months	4
Don't know	5

27

Q10 **For each of the following possible periods for consideration and reflection, should it be <u>possible</u> to reduce it?**
PLEASE CIRCLE ONE ANSWER FOR EACH PERIOD BELOW AT Q10

	Yes	No	Don't Know	
A period of six months	1	2	3	28
A period of 12 months	1	2	3	29
A period of 18 months	1	2	3	30
A period of 24 months	1	2	3	31

Q11 PLEASE ANSWER Q11 IF YOU SAID `YES' TO ANY PERIOD AT Q10

In what circumstances should this reduction be allowed? PLEASE CIRCLE AS MANY AS APPLY AT Q11 BELOW

The court should have the power to
reduce whatever the circumstances 1

To minimise the suffering to the
children 2

Other circumstances (PLEASE WRITE IN) 3

....

Don't know 4   32

Q12 **In what circumstances, should there be power to <u>extend</u> the period, if any?** PLEASE CIRCLE AS MANY AS APPLY

Children's welfare 1
Financial provision 2
Property ownership 3
Other circumstances (PLEASE WRITE IN) 4   33/34

....

Q13 ALL RESPONDENTS PLEASE ANSWER Q13

**Should the making of final arrangements for the matters listed below be a pre-condition of a divorce being granted
or not?** PLEASE CIRCLE AS MANY AS APPLY AT Q13

Arrangements for children 1
Financial arrangements 2
Property/Accommodation arrangements 3
Other arrangements (PLEASE WRITE IN) 4   36/37

....

Q14 **In what circumstances, if any, should the court be able to bar a divorce?** PLEASE WRITE IN

....   (38)

....   (39)

....

Q15 **Do you think judicial separation should be retained for those who do not want a divorce?** PLEASE CIRCLE ONE
ANSWER

Yes 1
No 2
Don't know 3   40

Q16 And do you think the laws and procedures relating to judicial separation should be kept in line with those relating to divorce law? PLEASE CIRCLE ONE ANSWER AT Q16 BELOW

Yes, in line with those relating to divorce law 1
No, keep it separate 2
Don't know 3   41

FAMILY MEDIATION

Q17 Turning to the subject of family mediation, taking into account the various advantages and disadvantages claimed for mediation, do you think it should be introduced with a reformed system of divorce or kept separate? PLEASE CIRCLE ONE ANSWER AT Q17 BELOW

Yes, introduced 1
No, kept separate 2
Don't know 3   42

Q18 PLEASE ANSWER Q18-Q21 IF YOU THINK MEDIATION SHOULD BE INTRODUCED WITH A REFORMED SYSTEM OF DIVORCE

You said that mediation should be introduced with a reformed system of divorce. In what ways, if any, can mediation be used to maximise the personal and economic well-being of the separating couple and their children? PLEASE WRITE IN

. . . . (43)

. . . . (44)

. . . .

Q19 In your opinion, is there a case for making mediation a compulsory step in the divorce process or not? PLEASE CIRCLE ONE ANSWER AT Q19 BELOW

Yes 1
No 2
Don't know 3   45

Q20 Should discussions between the parties during mediation be kept private (i.e. privileged), and not be disclosed to a court if mediation fails? PLEASE CIRCLE ONE ANSWER AT Q20 BELOW

Should not be disclosed, even if mediation fails 1
Should be disclosed if mediation fails 2
Don't know 3   46

Q21 PLEASE ANSWER Q21 IF YOU THINK DISCUSSION SHOULD BE PRIVILEGED.

If discussions remain privileged, should the mediator be allowed to inform the authorities if matters disclosed indicate that a child is being harmed? PLEASE CIRCLE ONE ANSWER AT Q21 BELOW

Yes 1
No 2   47

Q22 ALL RESPONDENTS PLEASE ANSWER Q22

Turning to the initiation of the divorce process, in your opinion, do you think there should be a single port-of-call for everyone wishing to initiate the divorce process, and if so, should it involve a personal interview? PLEASE CIRCLE ONE ANSWER AT Q22 BELOW

No 1
Yes
With personal interview 2
Without personal interview 3
Don't know 4   48

Q23 PLEASE ANSWER Q23-Q24 IF YOU THINK A PERSONAL INTERVIEW SHOULD BE INVOLVED.

What kinds of information should be offered in the initial interview? PLEASE CIRCLE AS MANY AS APPLY AT Q23 BELOW

Information about marriage guidance 1
Information about mediation 2
Information about divorce law 3
Information on procedure for getting divorced 4
Information on welfare and tax matters 5
Other (WRITE IN) 6

. . . .   49

Q24 **And in your view, how should this information be provided?** PLEASE CIRCLE AS MANY AS APPLY

In leaflets 1
In a single pack of information 2
On a video 3
Other (WRITE IN) 4   50

. . . .

Q25 ALL RESPONDENTS PLEASE ANSWER Q25

Please indicate whether you agree or disagree with the following statement. PLEASE CIRCLE ONE ANSWER AT Q25 BELOW

	Agree	Disagree	Neither/ Don't know
It should be possible for a divorcing couple who have mediated issues in dispute to obtain advice from the <u>same</u> solicitor	1	2	3 51

Q26 **During the divorce process, do you think the court should or should not verify the arrangements the couple are making for a life apart?** PLEASE CIRCLE ONE ANSWER AT Q26 BELOW

Should 1
Should not 2
Don't know 3   52

Q27 **Should the final arrangements made by a couple be approved by a court?** PLEASE CIRCLE ONE ANSWER AT Q27 BELOW

Yes 1
No 2
Don't know 3   53

Q28 **Finally, do you have any other comments to make?** PLEASE WRITE IN.

. . . . (54)

. . . .

. . . . (55)

. . . .

. . . . (56)

. . . .

To help us analyse the returns, please complete the following.

Q29   **Are you...?** PLEASE CIRCLE ONE ANSWER ONLY

Male 1
Female 2   57

Q30   **How old are you?** PLEASE CIRCLE ONE ANSWER ONLY

18-24 1
25-34 2
35-44 3
45-54 4
55-64 5
65+ 6   58

Q31   **Are you...?** PLEASE CIRCLE ONE ANSWER ONLY

Single 1
Married 2
Separated 3
Divorced 4
Widowed 5   59

Q32   **Age of your children.** PLEASE CIRCLE AS MANY AS APPLY

5 or under 1
6-10 2
11-18 3
Over 18 5
No children 6   60

NAME . . . .

ADDRESS . . . .

. . . .

. . . .

THANK YOU FOR TAKING THE TIME TO COMPLETE THIS QUESTIONNAIRE.

Bibliography Appendix C

Brannen, J. and Collard, J. (1982) *Marriages in Trouble, The Process of Seeking Help.*

Burgoyne, J. (1984) *Breaking Even: Divorce, Your Children and You.*

Church of England (1988) *An Honourable Estate, The Doctrine of Marriage According to English Law.*

Cockett, C. and Tripp, J. (1994) *Family Breakdown and its Impact on Children.* Exeter University.

Compass Partnership (1990) *The Public Cost of Separation and Divorce and the Cost Benefit of RELATE's Work.*

Conciliation Project Unit (1989) *Report to the Lord Chancellor on the Cost Effectiveness of Conciliation in England and Wales.*

Cummings, E. M. and Davis, P. (1994) *Children and Marital Conflict: The Impact of Family Dispute and Resolution.*

Davis, G. (1988) *Partisans and Mediators, The Resolution of Divorce Disputes.*

Davis, G., Cretney, S. and Collins, J. (1994) *Simple Quarrels - Negotiating Money and Property Disputes on Divorce.*

Davis, G. and Murch, M (1988) *Grounds for Divorce.*

Dominion, J., Mansfield, P., Dormor, D. and McAllister, F. (1991) *Marital Breakdown and the Health of the Nation, One Plus One.*

Dunlop, R. (1993) *Long-Term Adjustment of Children of Divorce: A Ten Year Study, Lecture presented at the National Family Court Conference, Sydney.*

Eekelaar, J. (1991) *Regulating Divorce.*

Eekelaar, J. (1994) *Family Justice: Ideal or Illusion?* (Lecture given in Current Legal Problems, 24 November).

Fisher, T. (1992) *Family Conciliation within the UK, Policy and Practice,* Second Edition.

Fricker, N. and Walker J. (1994) *Alternative Dispute Resolution: State Responsibility or Second Best?* Civil Justice Quarterly.

Funder, K., Harrison, M. and Weston, R. (1993) *Settling Down,* Australian Institute of Family Studies - Monograph 13.

Goode, W. J. (1993) *World Changes in Divorce Patterns.*

Haynes, J. (1993) *Alternative Dispute Resolution, The Fundamentals of Family Mediation.*

Ingleby, R. (1992) *Solicitors and Divorce.*

Kiernan, K. (1992) *The Impact of family disruption in childhood and transitions made in young adult life,* Demography.

Law Commission (1966) *Reform of the Ground for Divorce - The Field of Choice,* Law Com. 6.

Law Commission (1988) *Facing the Future - A Discussion Paper on the Ground for Divorce,* Law Com. 170.

Law Commission (1990) *The Ground for Divorce,* Law Com. 192.

Legal Aid Board (1994) *Annual Report 1993-94, Report to the Lord Chancellor on the Operation and Finance of the Legal Aid Act 1988.*

Lord Chancellor's Department (1993) *Looking to the Future - Mediation and the Ground for Divorce.* Cmnd 2424.

Marlow, L. (1990) *Conflicting Interests.* In: *The Handbook of Divorce Mediation.*

National Association of Family Mediation and Conciliation Services, (1994) *Annual Report 1994.*

NCH (1991) *Children Come First, The Case for Conciliation.*

Phillips, R. (1988) *Putting Asunder, A History of Divorce in Western Society.*

Putting Asunder - A Divorce Law for Contemporary Society (1966). The Report of a Group appointed by the Archbishop of Canterbury in 1964.

Rae, M. (1995) *A Proactive Court for Ancillary Relief Cases.* Family Law.

Rae, M. (1995) *Affidavits of Means - Past their Sell-by Date?* Family Law.

Utting, D. (1995) *Family and Parenthood - Supporting Families, Preventing Breakdown.* Joseph Rowntree Foundation.

Utting, D., Bright. J. and Henricson, C. (1993) *Crime and the Family, Improving Child-Rearing and Preventing Delinquency.*

Wadsworth, M., Maclean, M., Kuh, D. and Rodgers, B. (1990) *Children of Divorced and Separated Parents: Summary and Review of Findings from a Long-Term Follow-Up Study in the UK, Family Practice Vol 7 No 1.*

Walker, J., McCarthy, P. and Timms, N. (1994) *Mediation: The Making and Remaking of Co-operative Relationships.* Relate Centre for Family Studies - Newcastle University.

Walker, J. (1994) *Looking to the Future - Mediation and the Ground for Divorce.* Civil Justice Quarterly.

Walker, J. (1995) *Looking to the Future - Divorce and Alternative Dispute Resolution.* Paper presented at the Council of Europe 3rd European Conference on Family Law, Cadiz, April.

Wallerstein, J. S. and Kelly, J. B. (1980) *Surviving the Breakup, How Children and Parents Cope with Divorce.*

Printed in the United Kingdom for HMSO
Dd 0509937, 4/95, C35, 51-1304, 21159